FINDING

GRACE

IN LIFE

AND

DEATH

A BOOK FOR THE GRIEVING PARENT

978-0-692-83449-7

Printed by CreateSpace, an amazon.com Company

Graphic Design by
Johnson Printing & Graphics
Eliot, Maine

Scripture is taken from the King James Version
which is public domain.

Book is available at www.CreateSpace.com/6861806,
other retail outlets, amazon.com and other book
stores.

"In Memory of my daughter, Amazing Grace Browning, who touched our lives with purpose and perfection. "Thank you, for being mine."

-mom-

3

CONTENTS

INTRODUCTION

Perhaps there is no grief like that of the loss of a child. Perhaps. So then, perhaps you and I have experienced a depth of grief like no other. I think I know what the deepest and darkest moaning cry sounds and feels like. I know what it is like for a mother to grieve her child.

It isn't natural to have felt this loss, or to have suffered this pain. I can think of a million horrific things I would have rather endured. When I had first become a mother in 1998, my greatest fear was to lose my child. Now, nearly 20 years later, I'm writing about the loss of a child. The grieving. Yes, I too, have faced that. I own that horrendous "t-shirt" stained with fear, washed in tears and dried in grief. Who deserves this? I ask God, "What did I do to deserve this?"

People say, "God will never place on you what you can't handle." What the heck is that supposed to mean —— exactly? I can tell you that several years removed from her death, that He did allow something in my life that I personally couldn't handle. I was strong, but not that strong. I couldn't handle this ALONE!

The bond between a mother and child is like no other bond we experience here on earth. I'm not sure exactly how that bond is formed. Could it be that we carry a child inside of us in such a personal, endearing way that it reaches a greater depth, or is it a bond placed by God Himself when He created mankind? I don't have that answer, but I know the bond is real. I have possessed it since I first experienced the full effect of motherhood in August of 1998.

Before my first child was born, I knew I loved her, but the fullness of that love when I held her in my arms for the first time was precisely perfect love! I instantly had this amazing, never-before, out of this world bond with her! Although I have a very deep and singularly, special love with my husband, I didn't have that powerful bond the instant I met him. It grew stronger over time. However, with each of my children that bond came instantaneously. The love came the moment I recognized that a life was growing inside me, and the bond between us was formed the moment we met.

The bond carries a deep sense of emotional debt. I owe this child love. I owe them my sincerest devotion. I owe them sleepless nights, faithful care and tender kisses. I owe them my life. WHY? Because they are a gift from God! Yes, the same God I still question about the death of my child, did give me each of my children. What precious gifts!

Motherhood is a responsibility I owe to my children and to God. He gave me these beautiful, priceless gifts! It is my duty to tend to these lovely treasures as He would have me. I couldn't have peace, joy and happiness in my life without fulfilling my duty as a mother! It is my way of thanking Him for such blessings bestowed upon me: I tend to these precious jewels! I would be a miserable mess if I didn't fulfill such a high calling as "mom". But it is that calling that has now filled me with both the greatest joy and the deepest grief. My heart is full and empty all at once. It is happy and sad, altogether. It is complete, yet restless. It is free, but imprisoned by pain that only a grieving parent knows. Only a parent who has buried a child.

This book is my personal attempt to help other grieving parents through the expression of my own thoughts in the grieving of my child. It is full of both raw unfiltered emotion while at the same time, Heaven's joy and peace. This is my journey to "Finding Grace In Life And Death," a book for the grieving parent. I pray you will gain exactly what you need through its pages and let go of what you may. My deepest sympathy to each of you.

CHAPTER 1

FAITH

Oh, the times I have felt completely and utterly out of control! I have had such moments of extreme and untamed rage rush through me that I could just scream!!! It is like every fear and every heart-shattering moment I have ever felt in my entire life is felt in one moment of time. A moment that I am grateful is, somehow, brief and I'm able to gather my senses.

Those moments feel like a tingling heat going through my body. I literally have felt it in the tips of my fingers and toes! Physical heat. It is a burning of my heart and my emotions that sends a shock wave through me mentally and seemingly physically, too. For that brief moment, I feel mad. Not mad as in, angry mad, but *looney* mad!! CRAZY!! At that moment, I am the "psycho-est" of the psychopath, the "fridgid-est" of the bi-polar maniac and the "depress-est" of the depressed. Who would have thought such a disgusting madness could ever pass through me so erratically and without warning?

Then, as quickly as it comes ——— I gather myself together. I pick-up my grief-shattered heart and mend up my wounds. Tears flood me. I contain what my heart wants to release! It's better that way. I again manage my grief and gather understanding of who I am and who God is. I yield it back to Him. I surrender. I raise up my white flag as I lay there motionless again, wore out from the fight. I couldn't win, anyway. What is winning in this? What would it be? To have my child back here to be, who? Someone else? She has already lived the life intended for her. She fulfilled all of her life's purpose.

I go to God and say, "I know you have this big plan that is beautiful and great ——— I believe that! I do, but did it all really have to go down like this?" I can see myself pleading to Him, and I picture Him in a white robe sitting on a throne. I don't see a face, just a figure of a face. Most everything there is a bright, white color. I'm standing in front of Him, bold as ever, with angry tears and I'm looking Him square in the face and demanding Him for an answer. Questioning Him. "Why, God? Why me? Why my life? WHY MY CHILD and ——— Why like that?"

The questions flood my mind as reasoning dissolves. He just seems to stare back at me so kind, loving and good. He waits for me to just stop, and He just waits for me to finish my complaint. He allows me to vent my rant while He just waits ———

I notice the sandals on His feet. His feet are like mine. His sandals are the only color I see in the space of heaven I have found myself in, begging the question, "why?" His sandals are neutral in color, and it's just me and Him. I am aware Christ is present, but I don't see Him as I am toe to toe with God the Father. It's God that I demand an answer. I know He has control over all things. He is the giver and taker of all life and He took my little girl. Not only did He take her but He allowed her to live a life that included suffering. A life that most would say had no quality. So, "Why, God? Just tell me, why! Don't I, as her mother, deserve an answer from You?"

He waits. I feel the presence of love surrounding me. He has this presence of love and calm, while I am completely feeling angry and irrational! I am broken! Sad! CRAZY MAD!!! He is patient with me. He knows I'm venting. In fact, He knows and understands my pain. He knows I already trust His Plan, but at that moment —— I am struggling and questioning Him, again. For it is Grief and Rage that have visited me, yet again.

I look to Him for more understanding. "God, I need more understanding!" He waits. He is quiet. Then, through the passing of thought and time, I fall to my knees. My hands reach out and grab His ankles. I weep at His feet. I whisper, "Lord, I trust you. I don't know exactly why, right now, but I do trust You.

If it were not for You, she would have not been my child. Without You she would have not been known or had an existence. If it were not for You, I would have felt no love in my heart for her nor experienced the joy a child brings. Without You, I could never see her again. I know you love me, God. This just hurts, really badly! I hurt and I'm angry with You because I know you could have done something! I don't understand why it had to be this way! I do somehow believe that You have a bigger plan and I choose now to trust You. I surrender all of me."

Finally, my mind, heart and body are still. Calm. Comforted. The pain is still present but it does not singe my heart as did the burning of bitter rage. Trusting is easy once we give in to it. It's the getting there, the letting go, that is so difficult. Getting to that place of acceptance in a painful life circumstance. Trusting God with a life plan in which we can not see the end result. How can we find understanding in pain and death when we are not getting a clear answer as to why He allowed it? We want to see visually *why*. To completely know the reason *why*. We want to hear Him audibly speak to us and tell us *why* He allowed this. We want Him to give us a visual movie painted in the heavens with a clear storyline that gives us a good understanding of *why*? When we don't get that, we are forced to live by what is called *faith*.

Faith doesn't come naturally to us. We have to work at it. Give in to it. Yield to it. Surrender to the knowledge that we are NOT God and we indeed do not have all the answers. We can't see Him with our physical eyes and yet we are to trust His plan. Believing in something we can not see, that is faith. Trusting God and having faith in Him during times of great darkness is an undeniable challenge.

Having faith in God and His Heavenly Home when our ninety-eight year old grandmother ——– dies comes a whole lot easier, doesn't it? We seem to accept death when it comes at a time of what we would consider to be more *timely*. Anyone living to be ninety-eight years old has lived such a long life and now she's in heaven, praise the Lord! It's much easier to practice and surrender to God's plan through faith at a time like that, isn't it? She will certainly be missed, but we accept this death much easier. It's not too much of a challenge to express our faith. We talk about heaven and welcome the talks about God and His Plan. We find it more acceptable because we recognize the lengthy lifetime grandmother was given. Bless her heart, she was ready to go! She was tired of living! We will praise God during such a time because we find Him so good to have given her such a long life and now He has given her a brand new home in heaven, too. Oh, God is good at this time of life, isn't He?

But what about my baby girl? What about my faith when my child dies or is given a terrible diagnosis? What about the *untimely* death? What about our faith then?

I remember speaking to a man several years ago in a neighborhood not far from my home. He was really struggling with faith in God and why it is that faith was necessary for him to go to heaven one day. Possibly his struggle with faith in God was an untimely death of someone he loved. I don't know the reason. He never shared a reason and I have not spoken to him since; I don't even know his name.

However, in the course of our conversation that evening in his driveway, I remember sharing something with him about faith. I said something like this, "Ya know, I have never seen the brakes on my van. I don't know for certain they are actually there since I have not physically seen them with my eyes, but I *trust* they are there and that they are working properly each time I drive it. If I didn't trust that I had brakes on my van, I wouldn't drive it! That is faith. I use faith everyday without realizing it. Practicing faith in God is much the same; believing or trusting He is there without actually seeing Him face to face. Certainly if we could see Him with our eyes, we wouldn't doubt our Big God with

16

a Mighty Plan! If we could just see Him, but then *faith* wouldn't be necessary. It wouldn't even exist. It wouldn't be real. It wouldn't be *faith*." When I left the man's driveway that day it was evident to me that he understood some things more clearly. The man's faith had been increased that day.

Why then is faith necessary? Why does the Bible say, "...without faith it is impossible to please Him (God)..." that verse in Hebrews 11:6 goes on to say "...that He is a rewarder to them that diligently seek Him." Could it be that without faith, we wouldn't seek God? Makes perfect sense to me that if God were visible to my eyes and speaking to me audibly, I wouldn't need to seek Him out. James 4:8a says, "Draw nigh to God, and He will draw nigh to you..." What is it about seeking God and drawing close to Him that is so pleasing to Him? Why does God want little ol' Heather Browning from a cornfield town in Indiana to seek Him? The God of Heaven wants me to seek and draw close to Him? And in return, He will draw close to me? When I move towards God, He then moves closer to me? Why? God owns everything and has all power within His hands, so why would He want me? Why would He be moved by me? Why would He want to be close to me? That answer is found in Who God really is.

John 3:16 says, "For God so loved the world, that He gave His only begotten Son, that whosoever believeth in Him should not perish, but have everlasting life." God loves the people of this world. Why does He love all the people? I John 4:8b says it, "...for God is love." Quite simply, God is love. He is the definition and fullness of true, genuine, real love. Therefore, God loves the people! Each and every person in the world is loved by the Creator. He created you. He loves you because He is love. What is love? I Corinthians 13 tells us that love is kind. Love suffers long. Love thinks no evil. Love endures all things and never fails. That's just a portion of what love is and that's what God is because **He is LOVE**!

If we were all programed by God, The Creator, to seek Him and draw close to Him, could we truly then have real *faith*? If we could see God and know He was there or even hear His audible voice, would we then believe through *faith*? If God didn't choose by His Own Will to love us and prove it by sending His Son, would we have experienced His love? Could we have known what love really is without Christ? Could we ourselves have loved anyone else if we weren't first loved by Him? Scripture tells us that, "We love Him, because HE first LOVED us." - I John 4:19. He loved us by sending His Son to die for us. Jesus paid the debt for all of our sin.

Can love be love if it wasn't expressed with some type of acton? **Even in relationships, love is best expressed when it is challenged.** It is easy to express love when someone is easy to love, but when they challenge that love by some ill action —— —— that is when it is difficult to love them back. That's a "God" kind of love; loving others when they don't deserve to be loved.

If love is best expressed when it is challenged, is faith also best expressed when it is challenged? Maybe that is why God said in His Word, "But without faith it is impossible to please Him: for he that cometh to God must believe that He is, and that He is a rewarder of them that diligently seek Him." -Hebrews 11:6. Faith isn't faith at all without the lack of something; therefore allowing the ability to gain something, and love isn't love without it's lack of to prove its merit! Love is best expressed when it is given in response to someone who didn't earn it or doesn't deserve it. That's what God does for us. He is love for us and to us! We can return that love to God through our faith in Him.

What about my little girl? My precious daughter, Grace Browning. Well, it has been by a great challenge of my genuine faith in God that I have been able to express my trust and therefore my love to Him. Each time Grace visited death, before she fully experienced it, I was able to show my faith in God and my love towards Him. It was a very dark time, but I trusted Him.

19

I can not say that I never questioned Him. I questioned Him, many times! I definitely had my moments when I was pushed to my limits and beyond. So, what is a mother's limit? It rests in a mother's love. The deeper her love, the farther she is pushed during these times. The deeper the love, the greater the pain. I should know.

I remember the first time (in all of this) that I realized what faith can do when you are in a moment of great fear. There were many of those moments throughout Grace's time with us, but the first time I recall was the day I was visiting in the NICU (Neonatal Intensive Care Unit). My husband was working and I was there when, suddenly, Grace's stats dropped. Her oxygen level dropped into the teens! Nurses and doctors rushed to her side and began working on her. I stepped out of the way. A hospital staff member came to me and asked if I was okay. They asked if I wanted to step out or stay. I wanted to stay.

I stood, helplessly, watching them, and I realized that she could die and there was not a thing I could do! She may die right now, in front of me, is what I was thinking! It was in that moment that the fear of death really *hit* me. It *hit* me hard! I didn't want her to die! I didn't want to let her go! I felt this looming, dark fear come over me. Was she about to die right in front of me with all of this trauma going on? Surely it isn't supposed to be like this!!!!

I began to speak to God, immediately! "Oh God, help her! Heal her! Please let us keep her! Please don't take her home, God! Not like this! Please, not like this!! Surely, not like this!! God, if you are going to take her, please don't do it like this! God, please, not like this and not, today! I trust what You choose." I stood there and watched and prayed.

By the end of my prayer, her stats had come up. Within minutes, she regained her usual color. She looked herself again. She was back with us for the time-being though she was at death's door just minutes before. I wondered what God's plan was to be for her life? I believed with all of my heart that He could heal her. I knew He was listening to the prayers of so many by giving us this time, but what was His plan for her? Was He going to heal her or take her home? And when?

Living by faith wasn't easy. There seemed to be no understanding. There was no audible voice telling me that everything was going to be okay. I know that each life has purpose and she was sent to us for a purpose, God's purpose. I knew He had control over everything and though I didn't like how His Plan was unfolding, I lived by faith and trusted Him! I trusted Him with one of my dearest possessions in life! I trusted Him with Grace's life! I couldn't see God, but I was certain He was there. I was confident He knew what He was doing, though I'm only human and I had many times of doubt. In the end, I chose faith.

Those days were full of grim reports and daily visits to the brink of death for our little Grace. My faith was being challenged at it's max! Still I chose to live by complete faith in God even though the mental struggles through those challenging days were very real. Fear and death, frequently, visited us. When the evidence of distress presented itself, I fought; sometimes by faith and sometimes with my own strength. I questioned God at times, but then would remember who I am and Who He is! I had two choices: yield to God or fight, in my own strength, a loosing battle. I could have fought Him! He's given me a free-will to do so. I had freedom to curse Him, to turn away from Him and tell Him that I no longer believed He was good. In many ways, I did do that! But in the end of the struggles, I still chose faith.

Because of faith, I knew that God was working something beautiful that I simply couldn't see at the time. Through faith I knew that if He would not choose to heal her, He was still my God and He was still good. He was still worthy of my praise! So, each day while visiting Grace, I would praise God in song! Grace loved to hear me sing and this one particular song that I sang everyday became an understood between Grace and I. It was **our song** of praise together to God, and though she couldn't physically sing it with me, I knew that she was praising Him, too! She made it evident to me that she was listening and praising!

In the darkest of the dark, chains are lifted and burdens are freed when we yield our souls to an Almighty God in praise. I should know. I waited daily by the bedside of the sweetest, little, baby girl who was living on life support. I watched her squirm in pain and labor to breathe as I stood there, helpless. Though I desired greatly to fix every problem she had, I couldn't do it. I would have gladly given my own life to save her life! Even now, as I write, tears flow and that same passion to save her life floods over me. I wanted to save her! I wanted Him to save her! I wanted Him to heal her!

Praising God brought me peace. He was still my God and He was still good.

I could either go crazy fighting God in a loosing battle or trust Him. Literally. I had these moments in my mind that were screaming in agony! It was as if I could hear myself scream a bloody scream! I was screaming for her! I was screaming to God, "Why won't you fix this? What purpose is this to have her here in this state? What possible good is being done here in this tiny box with her connected to all of this stuff preventing me from holding my dear girl in my arms? Why would you let such an innocent, little thing suffer for even a brief moment? This makes *no sense* to me!"

My faith was constantly being tested, but it was through faith that I yielded to His Will and found peace. Sometimes it was moment by moment that I was yielding to Him because moment by moment I experienced tragedy and fear by facing her death. Many of those moments were given over to a song of praise; a tear-streaming, peaceful song of praise. Yes, I went from great fear and pain to perfect peace in just moments. I yielded, trusted and praised Him! Faith brought about immediate peace and no matter what was happening at that very moment, if I yielded, I found ———— peace.

It was faith that got me through that time and it was faith that pleased God. Faith that He had given to me. Not a faith I possessed on my own. I loved my little Grace so very deeply all of her days because God loved me first. I have *love* because He loves. Love originated through the Father Who sent His Son. I have faith because the Son pleased the Father through His action of *faith* to give of Himself as a sacrifice to all mankind! I have love and I have faith because of Him!

Though the deep love that I had and still have for my dear Grace can not be physically seen by others, it can be experienced by the actions I took and even the passion in the words I write now. Though the faith that I have in my Jesus also can not be physically seen, it can be experienced as something real and evident in my life through my actions; especially in the most challenging of times! When we believe in something or someone we can not see ——- that is faith! Surely if I can place some faith in the brakes on my vehicle without actually seeing them there each and every time I go to drive it, I can at least muster up even a small amount of faith in God during the good times and the bad times. A little faith in a BIG GOD can go a long, long way!

Beautiful evidences of real faith is shared at times of great sorrow. I have been able to express my strongest faith during my greatest times of weakness. Here is a poem that I wrote at a time when my faith was being challenged in the death of our daughter:

"God, What Were You Thinking?"

God, what were You thinking when you sent her here

to take her and leave us so painfully drear?

Her days were so dark yet beautifully shared,

25

With a life meant to make it's presence loud said.

She spoke not a word, yet she taught us so well,

How peace and contentment are ours if we dwell:

Of a place, of a home we shall one day see,

If I trust of the promise You made to me.

God, what were You thinking when You saw her in pain?

When her breaths were so shallow and burdened, insane!!!

God, what were You thinking in all the times I would pray,

"LORD, PLEASE NEVER TAKE MY CHILDREN AWAY...?"

And what were You thinking when little hearts and hands,

Said good-bye to a sister with tears I just couldn't stand????

God, please tell me what You were thinking

when I believed with all faith,

You could heal her with just one touch of Your grace.

If all life is within and under Your control,

Why wouldn't You heal her and save that dear soul?

And just ——-

WHAT WERE YOU THINKING, when You sent such a Son,

Who was more innocent than my dear little one,

To be mocked, shattered, beaten and torn:

To benefit me, The sinful one?

So, I don't know why or even how,

Your infinite mercy and peace have allowed

me to trust You and yield to Your marvelous grace.

FOR It's Your truth and Your love that have kept me *in place!*

So, what were You thinking of me on that day;

You watched Your Son die in a far worse way?

And yet in Your Power and Heavenly Might,

it was needed to change the course of ALL LIFE!

What were You thinking? I'm sure I will see ———-

one day ———- just why You gave her ———- HIM ———- to me.

Until then I will still praise Your name!

For heaven and earth is Yours to maintain.

Me, I'm just some bones and some flesh.

It's You Who gave me life with Your breath.

Now, each time I feel so desperately low

and fail to see the gifts you bestow;

I'll remember to think of this one little phrase ———-

"God, what were you thinking?"

So, Your name I will praise!

FAITH MAKES IT POSSIBLE TO PRAISE and TRUE PRAISE WILL BRING RICH PEACE.

CHAPTER 2

THERE'S ALWAYS KETCHUP

Our daughter, Amazing Grace Browning, was born in a twin pregnancy. Her twin bother's name is Wesson Gauge Browning. We delivered them on April 27, 2013. Both were born with heart defects and needed open-heart surgery.

Our daughter, Grace, had a chromosome abnormality called Trisomy 18 (Edwards Syndrome). Her twin brother, Gauge, has Trisomy 21 (Downs Syndrome). Our daughter lived 61 days. She died on June 27, 2013. Her brother, Gauge, was released from Neonatal Intensive Care (NICU) when he was 47 days old, on June 13, two weeks before Grace died. His heart surgery was being planned but he needed to gain weight before surgery so he was sent home with us until that time came.

About nine or ten days after we buried Grace, Gauge became ill and was back in the same hospital that his twin sister had just passed away in. Our son was sick. He had some respiratory issues related to a virus. He was in the hospital on oxygen and some medications. It was unclear when he would go home, although it was expected for him to fully recover.

As I sat there with him in the hospital I began to feel very discouraged and heavy-hearted! Having just gone through such a time of tragedy, I desired nothing more than to be at home with my grieving family. However, being back in the same hospital with a sick child made it seem impossible to get beyond everything. The season of hardship was still present in our lives.

My husband was home with our five other children. We had all just buried our little Grace. I wanted to be home with them during this time helping to bring them comfort. We needed Gauge at home helping to fill the void we were experiencing in Grace's death, but Gauge was back in the hospital and all the turmoil continued.

The months of great heaviness were turning into months and months. I wondered why we couldn't have it easy for just a little while. I sat there eating a lunch that had been brought in to me by the hospital staff (chicken fingers, fries and mac'n'cheese) my favorite there. I tore open a package of ketchup and dipped-in my fries. I took that first bite of those toasted and salty potatoes dipped in that sweet and tangy ketchup thinking to myself, "There's always ketchup."

I was sitting there eating one of my favorite meals, complete with the perfect dipping sauce for my delicious, carbo-hydrated *friends*. I found comfort in the taste and texture of my food! Who was I to have such a meal when countless others in other countries today will have nothing, not even clean water! I began to be thankful. My son Gauge was still living. My wonderful husband and children were safe in a home full of love. I remember taking a hard swallow as the tears of joy filled my eyes. By the grace of God, I was able to see how good things really were despite that Grace was no longer with us and despite that I was sitting back in the same hospital with that same smell and feel! God was still good and I was able to see it through just a few of the blessings in my life that day! It started with the opening up of a simple package of ketchup, then dipping into and tasting one of my favorite things to eat!

I had watched my child suffer while fighting to live and she died in my arms just days before in that very hospital, a few floors below. But I had my son there alive having defeated so many obstacles already! I knew I had a wonderful family. I had a home that was furnished and comfortable. Clean water! Heating and Air! I had a vehicle to drive home and visit my family. I had clothing. I had taken a hot shower in the hospital that morning having freshened-up with my own cosmetics! I had

31

a loving, supportive husband. I had a strong and beautiful nearly fifteen year old daughter. I had a gorgeous and genuinely sincere thirteen year old daughter, a compassionate and darling eleven year old daughter, a handsome and compassionate nine year old son, a vibrant and happy four year old daughter and just feet away from me I had the twin brother of our little Grace. I had the support of hundreds and the prayers of thousands. I had Salvation. I had peace knowing I would see my daughter again. I had Jesus. I had hope, and I even had ketchup.

Many would say, "Curse God! Why would a loving God allow such tragedy?" I say, "Why would I doubt a God who created all life?" A God Who created this beautiful world with all of its sights and sounds. A God Who spoke into existence the fish of the sea, the fowl of the air and me. A God Who freely gave of His Own Son. A God Who desires to give each of us good things. A God Who sees the bigger plan I can not see. A God Who comforts. A God Who heals. A God Who made my daughter perfect. (It was Satan who gave the disease in her body. He is where the blame really lies.) God loved me enough that when He gave His Own and only Son to die for me, I was set completely free of all my sins. I'm free of all failure. I am cleansed of every stain and blot because of Him! That's what I say ——— and there's always ketchup. Ketchup to comfort my

32

body through it's sense of taste. The ketchup was exceptionally good that day as I began to see all that I truly had in life! My God-given sense of taste began a snowball of thanks for all that I really had!

It was God that gave me and you the sense of taste, feel and smell. It was He that gave us the ability to both laugh and cry: reaching depths of human emotions not seen to this extent in any other creature in all of the universe. Humans are pretty awesome! The depth of the emotions of mankind; what a powerful thing to possess. It was that power in the emotion of love that I had for my daughter which gave me the ability to feel something in my heart and soul so powerful, so unique and so beautiful.

The love between a mother and her child is a God-given love! (Could this be where the bond originates from? God?) When that love between a mother and her child is separated, a piece of core human bonding aches with emotions. Painfully and deeply, aches! The bond was never intended to be separated! It was not in God's plan!

Thousands of years ago, God created mankind, Adam and Eve. He had just completed Creation of all things including land, sea, animals, daylight and darkness. It was a beautiful, complete and peaceful place there in the Garden of Eden (the

33

place He had given them to live.) Air and water, with no impurities. Plants and trees of vibrant color and perfect detail. No creatures warring against another; not man, nor beast. It was complete serenity, with no sickness and no death. It was fresh, crisp and new; created by an Absolute and Perfect God! Oh, the sights there must have been there! I imagine heaven to be so much better! However, The Garden of Eden came closer to its beauty than anything we could ever see.

The Garden was simply marvelous until the event that changed the course of us all, the sin of mankind. The Bible says, "Wherefore, as by one man sin entered into the world, and death by sin; and so death passed upon all men, for that all have sinned:" (Romans 5:12) Because of the sin that occurred there, death is now experienced by all men. The garden had become tainted by sin. It was no longer perfect. The Garden of Eden was no longer a safe and peaceful place to be. It began to fill with weeds. Plants and food were no longer easily accessible. Man and woman noticed their nakedness. Sickness and disease began. Woman would soon travail with great pain in the delivery of her child. Man would work by the sweat of his brow in toil of the things needed to survive. Death also became a reality, and in every continent across the globe, fear now dwells in the hearts and minds of us all ——— the fear of losing someone in death.

34

Death is likely one of the things least spoken of in homes across the world. It is the "elephant in the room." It is evident and often times very present in some aspect of each of our lives. You can not pretend it or wish it away. We avoid speaking about it because it is entirely too heavy for us to carry. We can not imagine our lives without "so and so" nor the thought of living each day without them! How could we possibly? NO WAY! We think to ourselves, "There is just no way I can do it! I can't! I won't even think about it! I would die without them!" So, we don't speak about it. Just the thought of it is entirely too painful! (This is why many will turn to substance abuse or some other type of terrible and consuming behavior.) The thought of separation or the actual separation death brings to us is very taxing on one's emotions. Therefore, it is difficult to live life without them or think of living life without them so we avoid speaking about it.

Remember death was never meant to occur. God had no intentions of us ever experiencing death. It was and is the sin of mankind that has made it a reality in each of our lives today. So, why do we sin and why did God give mankind the ability to sin? Because He gave us the ability to choose. He gave us a free will. We can freely choose how to live our lives. He loved us that much!

He could have made us all to be robot-like, programmed to praise Him and live perfect lives without sin, but would that have been a *loving* God? If we were programmed to *be good,* could that be real, genuine *goodness*? If we were programmed to *love*, would that be real *love*? The answer to both questions would be an astounding, "NO!" Love isn't *love* without it's freedom to express it in limitless degrees nor is *good* truly righteous without it's independence. Love gives us the ability to prove outwardly what we profess to have for someone on the inside! It is when the emotion is expressed that it proves the evidence of something we can not actually see; we can only see the results of the love. Yes, we can see love present on the faces of those that are expressing it but what we see in that *look* is only evidence of the real love present on the inside of someone! Love is an emotion! It has freedom to express itself without any limits! It is individualized in each of us and that is the beauty of it! No programming! The real deal! God designed us that way because He loved us!

A loving God created mankind. He loved mankind so much that in all of His complete power, He gave us the ability to choose how we would live our life. *To choose how we would live and how we would love.* In that living comes relationships between people! In those relationships is love and sadly, many times, the lack of. God chose to give us that ability to choose! This was a deep expression of love on His part that can not be completely understood by us. We can't understand how God would give us a choice. If He indeed loves us, why would He allow us to make a choice that would cause us to end up not spending eternity in Heaven with Him? Why would He give us the freedom to sin? Why would He give us a choice to not love those we should love?

A mother should love her child! A father should love his son or daughter! **Why would He let us choose?** It is because He loves us so much and so deeply, He can first ——- *let go*! In all His power ——- He loved us enough that He gave us the ability to express real love by letting go of us! Love is love because of choice. It is real because of choice! If we were programed to love, what reward would we have? Would you feel loved if it were *forced* of someone to express it? Absolutely not!

The closest I can come, in my personal life, to understanding what it's like to love so deeply that you are able to *let go* is the day my husband and I both made a decision concerning our daughter Grace. Twenty-four hours before her death we had been given the knowledge that she had such a significant heart defect it could never be repaired. In that hour or possibly that very moment, we realized that we were now keeping her alive for us. It was no longer about fighting for her life and giving her a chance at living. It was now about us keeping her here for us; about our not having to let go! We didn't want to experience that death with it's depth of grief.

Once we realized that it was about keeping her here for us, we made the easiest and yet most difficult decision we have ever made! In love, we took her off of life support and let her go! God loves each of us to a much greater degree! He loves us as a father should love his child. He loves us so much, He let us go so we could receive what is best. It is best to have real and true love. It is best that we aren't all programmed to be exactly the same. It is best to have a free will of each our own. And it is best that Grace is now in Heaven and no longer suffers. Love.

In God's letting go we were all given the ability to express real, genuine love! Love isn't love without that choice nor would life be worth living without the freedom to choose how we want to live it! If you don't believe that, ask the guy spending life in prison. Ask him if he feels that he is able to really *live* while inside those prison walls! He can't live to the fullest because he can't love to the fullest! His relationships in life are greatly limited by those prison walls! He doesn't see the face of his loved ones lying next to him when he wakes up in the morning. He doesn't kiss his children "good-night." He is limited in life by his limited expressions of love.

God gives each of us the ability to choose how we express the depth of our love in relationships! God's love was selfless enough to give each of us power over our own lives; our own free will with its ability to do right or to do wrong, by choice. **God understands that without the option to choose, there is no such thing as real love or real faith!** That is where the beauty lies. When you can give-up your own personal desires in hopes to bring the best to someone else's life. That is love! And when you choose to do the right thing, even when you really want to do the wrong thing, that is faith!

Remember that Scripture says that God is love. He Himself —- IS —- Love! We are loved by Him and therefore we are able to love. Our love completely originates from Him! It is passed to us from His love for us. We are given the power to use that love as we will. We can love deeply or passively. We can love to the fullest or love at a minimum. However, God's love continues towards us to the same degree, even on our worst day. It was fully expressed to us on the Cross when Jesus paid our sin debt. *OUR* SIN DEBT!

Jesus did not have to go to the cross. He did not have to pay our debt, but He chose to pay it. That is love. He expressed

39

the love that He had for us on the cross when He chose (without obligation) to carry our shame and offer Himself as the sacrifice for our sin. That is a true expression of love. It is the model of what love is. The giving of self without any expectation of a return to those who do not deserve it. God continually offers His love to us. His love never fails and it never changes. Best of all, His love never lacks one single thing! It is always complete and always enough!

I think of the countless souls that God loved as His children who chose an eternal separation between themselves and God because of their lack of faith. What pain our Heavenly Father experiences in this separation between He and those He loves so deeply! He, in love, gave them that choice. That choice breaks His heart!

When we let our daughter go, our hearts were shattered because of love! We walked her to the gates of heaven and in our deep love for her, we let her go. It broke our hearts! Yes, love is best expressed when it is challenged! We chose to do what was best for her even though it brought the void we still feel to this day of not having her here with us! *We let her go* and it left a void in her absence that continues to break our hearts.

God gave me the ability to break His heart by giving me a choice of loving Him in faith or not! I have the choice to love Him back. His love for me is real, <u>therefore it does not pivot on my</u> <u>love or lack of love towards Him in return.</u> **He loves me even** **when I don't love Him back.** He continues to love me even when I angrily pour out my complaint to Him, He still loves me! The Bible says that we love Him because He first loved us! He let us go. His love for me has given me the ability to exemplify my faith in Him. I have faith in Him because of His love He proved for me on the cross of Calvary and *this GREAT LOVE* *prompts me to a true faith in a real God!* <u>This faith</u> allowed me to see, that day, sitting in the hospital with my son, all the wonderful blessings I had been given *by God* in my life! His love gave me faith. My faith gives me love and hope. Hope gave me *ketchup*. Faith caused me to see beyond the pain and fear that I was experiencing. It opened my eyes of appreciation and gratitude of God's love, my family and even ketchup! The real *ketchup* I was given and enjoying that day was the faith to see it was because of God's love for me that I was enjoying yet another moment in life! Though all around me seemed to be sorrow and fear, there was a great deal of evidence of bountiful blessings from God and I even had ketchup!

CHAPTER 3

THE BALANCING ACT

Our twins were born at 32 weeks and 2 days. Our son, Gauge, weighed 3 lbs. and 7oz. Our daughter, Grace, weighed 2 lbs. and 2oz. Both were delivered during an emergency C-section. Gauge began breathing on his own, but Grace did not. She was placed on a ventilator (life support).

Immediately after birth, the twins were placed into Neonatal Intensive Care (NICU) at Kosair Children's Hospital in Louisville, KY; this was about an hour drive from our home in Indiana. I quickly came to learn of families being separated for weeks and months or having to relocate temporarily due to their family's hardship of having a child or children under hospital care. Many of those families lived hours away and some from other states. I even heard of families traveling to this hospital from other countries! I felt so blessed just to be able to drive back and forth each day between home and the hospital. I was able to see all of my family members each day, but it became a balancing act like I had never learned before.

As I shared, previously, we had five other children at home and twins in the Intensive Care Unit at our local hospital. My husband and I began to learn what seemed to be the best way to tend to everyone in such a time of turmoil. My husband was self-employed. He owned and operated a local, used car lot that was struggling financially. He was torn between working long hours trying to provide for our family, keeping up with hospital visits and tending to me and the other children.

My husband's mother, Diane, lived three miles down the road, so she was with our children at home while my husband was running the business and I was at the hospital. My husband carried a great financial burden, but he was also carrying the fear of losing the twins, the emotional stress of watching his wife do her best to care for our seven children (two of which were in critical care) and this new balancing act of distributing his time between home, hospital and business. It was a heavy load just to carry one of these burdens! Many people crumble solely under the stress of a failing business. My husband had a failing business, critically ill twins and a wife and children who were all in great emotional distress! All the while, he himself was under significant turmoil, fear and heartache! On the other side, I can see that he was challenged the greatest during this time! We did lose our daughter and our business. Our twin-son, Gauge, did undergo his open-heart surgery when he was just six-months old. During the surgery he suffered a **severe** stroke. Life continued to throw punches that were life-changing; each deeply and painfully difficult.

Let me back up to tell you more of our lives before entering into such a season of tragedy. It all began the fall of 2012. I had recently decided to work on my health. I decided to watch my diet intake more carefully and I began running as a regular exercise. My mother had died of cancer at the age of fifty-two. I was thinking about how close I was starting to get to that age myself and I wanted to try to do what I personally could do to live a longer life.

I was out taking a run one morning in October of 2012 experiencing some great fatigue. I wondered why I couldn't do my usual run. Even if I felt sick or had not been getting enough sleep, I could usually run for a particular amount of time. As I thought deeper, I began to wonder, could I be pregnant? I was only able to run five minutes that day. I couldn't believe it! What was wrong with me?

When I returned home, I got into my vehicle, drove up to the local Dollar General store and bought the one-dollar pregnancy test. I came home, took the test and it was immediately positive! WHAT? NO-WAY! This can't be right! I had just turned thirty-six in August before finding out I was pregnant that October. My husband and I were not planning to have more children, but God had something else in mind. We were expecting, again.

During an ultra-sound at seven weeks of pregnancy we found out that we were having twins! HOLY MOLY! Then at seventeen weeks of pregnancy we found out that we were having boy/girl twins. At 19 weeks of pregnancy we found out that our girl twin may have a chromosome abnormality called Trisomy 18. If she had this birth defect it would be considered lethal.

As the weeks passed in the pregnancy, we found out that both of the babies had heart defects and there were more signs of our daughter having Trisomy 18. Those visits to the maternal fetal specialist were full of bad news. It seemed that each time we had an appointment we were getting worse and worse news of life-threatening complications for them and eventually a threat to my life as well. This began a season of troubles. Life began to bring about severe difficulties and it became very taxing to balance our everyday lives.

The twins were born. Our daughter was put on life support and lived all of her sixty-one days in the hospital. Nearly each day of her life she faced death, while we watched. Her brother spent forty-seven days in the Neonatal Intensive Care. He had his ups and downs but none of his challenging days, at that time, were nearly as significant as each day of our daughter's life. Our children at home were fearful of what was going to happen to our sweet Grace. We were all deeply troubled about what was going to happen.

We lived in a heavy and fearful unknown state of mind for many days. Long and difficult days. We were watching each other live heartache everyday while we lived it as well! One child dying, one in critical care and five other children, each at such a delicate age, living in an unforgiving storm of life. A mother painfully cautious of her brood; desiring so much to see everyone get through it alive and unscathed. A father trying to balance the home in a way no man should ever be required.

How would we get through this? Could we get through it without collateral damage? Was there a good balance? Could a positive outcome even be envisioned through such a time of fear and darkness?

Finding the balance that brings about the hope we were all looking for can be especially hard when you are facing a terminal diagnosis or death of close family members or friends. You feel lost. You can no longer think clearly. Your ability to reason

47

through the murky waters in this pool of muddy filth that life has dealt to you, is gone! How do you find a balance when you can't even think clearly?

How much time do you spend at the hospital with a dying child? How much time do you spend at home with your other children? How much time do spouses need to give to each other while still tending to the desperate needs of their family? How much time do you sleep? There simply isn't enough time! There is no perfect balance for these types of life circumstances!

My children at home needed me there to console them when I was at the hospital visiting the twins. My husband needed my advice with the decision making in the business while it suffered greatly. My twins needed to hear momma's voice and feel momma's touch. There were bills to pay, rides to and from school to arrange, grocery lists, school programs to attend, decisions to make in the health of not one but two of our children in critical care. Doctors calling; babies crying; momma crying; daddy crying; heads-spinning; emotions whirling; danger creeping around every corner of this massive, real-life, roller-coaster ride from the pits of Hell from Satan, himself!

What we needed was a balance. The scales of life were turned up-side-down! Everything was thrown into a tailspin

48

within minutes! WE HAD TO FIND A BALANCE AND FIND IT
QUICK!

I liken this balance we were looking for to the day I was
learning to ride a bicycle for the first time. When I was six years
old, my Aunt Joannie was teaching me how to ride her banana-
seat bike. She was just a few years older than I was, so her bike
was just the right size for me to learn on; I could reach the
pedals and handlebars just fine.

We were on my grandparents gravel driveway in
Georgetown, Indiana, on a perfect summer morning. Reflecting
on it now, I can almost smell the pasture where my grandfather
kept the family's pet cow, Maggie. It was there, in that rich,
country atmosphere, that my aunt was teaching me how to ride a
bicycle.

I remember trying and trying (again and again) to do what
my Aunt Joannie said. She kept saying, "Keep pedaling and
don't stop!" I would begin to pedal, and, as soon as, I could feel
her let go of the bike, I would stop pedaling, lose control of my
steering and fall down. I quickly learned to catch myself with my
foot so I wouldn't hit the gravel on my shins and knees.

I had a few minor cuts and scrapes. I remember getting
back on the bike after I had fallen once; I stopped and thought to
myself, "This time I'm going to just keep pedaling." I finally took

49

off riding into that sweet country air! I finally listened. I got over the fear of falling. I learned that if I would just keep pedaling, I could keep my balance on the bicycle and ride. Even when I did begin to fall, I learned how to stop the fall and keep on going.

Whatever life brings, we've got to keep pedaling in order to learn the right balance of whatever is new in our lives. What is new may not be welcomed because of how painful it is, but we must keep on pedaling. If we don't pedal, we fall; we get stuck and we don't move. We die as human beings. We forfeit our abilities to bring into this world the beautiful things each of our lives were meant to bring!

Your life's *ride* will be found in the balance that you learn by continuing to pedal on! If you fall, get back up and pedal again! Don't quit! **If you stay on the bike, you will find that God is holding that banana-seat!** He's holding on and He is not ever going to let go, so DON'T jump off! Don't quit! God's got your back!

The reason I learned how to find my balance when riding the bicycle that day was because I stopped and took an evaluation of my situation. I thought about it, jumped back on, pedaled while facing the fear of falling. That's how I learned how to find my balance. In life, whatever the situation, just stop and take mental note; then ride. Face the fears. Go. Live. In living and not quitting, you are working out a balance. Don't stop. Your life has greater purpose than you can imagine. **Don't Quit.**

Remember, you are not riding alone!

My husband and I decided at some point that no matter what ——- our marriage, our children, our home, our family and our live's were valuable enough to keep on pedaling through the muddy terrain! Sure, we thought about giving-up ——— many times. There were even times of deep sorrow and toil that in the moment, to some degree, we did stop pedaling. Once we stopped and took an evaluation, recognizing how beautiful our lives really were, we resumed our journey. ONWARD!! God held us then and He's got our back's now!

Each of us have a life to live and a mark on this world to leave! Keep pedaling! It will be the only way you will find the balance in your life that you so greatly desire to have! That balance brings peace and contentment! My family found that balance in our lives by continuing to pedal, knowing God had our back's! You may hit a rock or two, you may even be chased by the largest and most aggressive dog on the block and at times you will feel enormous fatigue, but don't stop! Don't quit! Just keep pedaling! You will get the right balance when you trust God to hold your seat! You, just pedal.

CHAPTER 4

IN EVERY THING, GIVE THANKS

"In every thing give thanks: for this is the will of God in Christ Jesus concerning you." I Thessalonians 5:18

Are you joking? Give thanks in everything? Surely God didn't mean that I should give thanks for a dying daughter, a sick son, a grief-stricken family, a stressed-out husband and my dear ol' broken heart! Oh, and the financial mess —— that too? Give thanks? Ha-Ha! Yeah, I'm gonna give thanks, alright!

Actually, I did. I gave thanks to God for her life, my son's life, for my life, my families live's and many more things. Why? Because I knew how good I really had it! Good? Yeah, good!

Today in countries all across this planet, many will search for a single meal. They will struggle to survive life just one more day. They will wear the same used clothing that was given to them possibly years ago. They will run dirt paths of a land desolate of food with no shoes on their feet; not *only* them, but everyone around them. They will watch their loved ones die of diseases. They will drink contaminated water. Little children will perform sexual acts with no one to deliver them; no one will fight for them. Who will allow them to do such? Oftentimes, their very own parents! Are you thankful, yet?

Just about seven decades ago, hundreds of thousands of families were ripped apart by the hatred of Adolph Hitler. Millions were killed in the most inhumane ways. Men, women and children were assaulted in horrific ways while their loved ones stood by and had to watch. Can you ———— just imagine? Mothers were suddenly and abruptly separated from their infants and children not knowing their fate or **even worse**, knowing their end. This was a time of suffering for countless humans on uncharted scales while most of the world turned an eye to it all! Unbelievable, isn't it?

Just a few thousand miles from us are people who live in fear of their lives everyday. They are surrounded by angry men. Their children can not play safely in their streets. The sounds of guns, bombs and violence in their cities on a regular basis. It is their everyday life. They have lost loved ones to a religious war they don't understand. They stay huddled in their houses in fear of being killed by a stray bullet or unexpected bombs targeted at someone else. Thousands upon thousands will be forced to relocate their families to a new land leaving nearly all of their personal possessions behind. Feeling thankful, yet?

Yes, dear people, I believe I will be thankful for the hot shower I had today and for the food that I will eat, today. Though my daughter is no longer here with me, she is in Heaven. My son was sick, needed a surgery, had a stroke during the surgery but I will still eat my "ketchup" and be thankful for it!

My family continued to be fed. Times were hard, but I knew I still had so many reasons to be thankful. I knew my life was blessed despite her death and the turmoil it was and is to live through it. I began to take notice of every detail of my life and it was then that I began to be overwhelmed with gratitude! I could still walk away from the freshly broken ground where my baby girl's body lay and thank God for what He had given me. I thanked Him for giving her *to me*. I thanked Him for her sixty-one days.

In every thing, I will give thanks. Why? Because I don't have to look too far to see how good my life has really been. I'm thankful to have been born in a country with as many common luxuries as we have in the U.S. Most people in this country have hot/cold fresh, running water and three meals each day.

Yeah, I was sitting in the hospital one day eating my toasty french-fries and ketchup with a smile on my face! Yes, I did. I had a smile on my face and a tear in my eye! GRATITUDE! THANKFUL! I even had an oder of hot, fried chicken fingers and the best dawg-on mac'n'cheese you've ever tasted to go along with those fries! Did I mention that the hospital my children were in even has a charity to help families in need? A hospital that also has funding available for families who don't have insurance or families that cannot afford to buy a meal or pay their bills during such times! Oh, and the Ronald McDonald house that is just a few blocks away from the hospital which provides housing for families who are having to relocate; housing with clean water, hot baths, play-rooms, beds and even their own little kitchenettes.

The hospital had a washer and dryer set for me to clean my laundry. I had family and friends that would visit often. A church family that provided meals at my home everyday for nearly two months! I could go on and on about the blessings we received and the blessings that were available had we needed them. We were in a painful season of life, but we had blessings all around us!

Mother's should be thankful to wash clothes because they actually have clothing for their families to wash. Father's should be grateful for his job because he can work to provide for his family! We are a minority in this world, the citizens of this country (USA), and we have more accessibility than any person of any other country in the world! Our families can receive a free high-school education and much financial aid is available to every citizen of this country who desires to further their education beyond high school. Momma can bathe her babies in a hot bathtub with soap and take them to receive medical care. Don't forget the vehicle(s) to transport to and from work, school, friends homes and hopefully church where you worship and thank your God for all the blessings He has bestowed upon you! Maybe you don't each of these blessings, but you do have many luxuries if you live in the United States! If you will see them in the large quantity they have been given, you too, will be thankful as I was that day I had ketchup to eat with my fries. You will be thankful in everything. Every. Single. Thing.

If I had no family, no food, no clean water, no shelter, no medical care and no safe place to live, I would still be blessed! I'm blessed regardless of my things because I have a Savior who has provided me a home in Heaven when my life here is over. This life here is short, but I will spend eternity there in Heaven. This life is brief; eternity is forever! I may end-up with nothing left here. I may even end-up living in fear and starving to death, but regardless of how my life here ends, I will have a new beginning in a place prepared for me by Jesus the King for all of eternity!

Heaven will one day be my forever place to dwell. Until then, I live temporarily in this temporary world full of temporary trials and temporary treasures. The only things I can take with me are those things that are eternal. People are eternal. My little Grace is eternal and I will see her again for all eternity!

I will never see any of my earthly things from here again (once I'm gone, that is.) Not even the little outfits that I hold so dear worn by my little Grace. I won't see or hold any of these things ever again. I once heard of a pastor using a sermon illustration in the church's parking lot as people drove by or came to church one Sunday. The illustration was a funeral home hearse towing a U-Haul trailer. It was parked out in front of the church's parking lot. A hearse, towing a U-Haul trailer. Picture that!

We can not take our earthly treasures with us. They are temporary, even these trials we face are temporary. Our lives here are what the Bible says, "…is even a vapor, that appeareth for a little time, and then vanisheth away." -James 4:14b. Our lives are temporary and pass quickly. As quickly as a vapor!

I can't say I understand God's Will for my life most of the time. I simply live by faith as much as I can. I can not see God's Will, but I choose to trust it because He is God. Even Jesus Christ, the only begotten Son of God, gave us an illustration of faith in trusting God's Plan for His life. In the accounts of Scripture as Jesus is just about to be captured by the Roman Soldiers and crucified, He is found praying in the Garden of Gethsemane. His prayer: "Saying, Father, if thou be willing, remove this cup from me: nevertheless not my will, but thine, be done." Luke 22:42 In this verse we find that even Jesus was troubled with what was happening in His life at that time. He acknowledges the Will of God for His life and says, "not my will, but thine, be done."

Jesus was troubled because His life was in jeopardy. He was about to face beatings and mockeries, pain and shame. He was about to be shredded apart physically while being mocked by those He loved. He would be nailed to a cross made of wood and hung to suffer an agony like no one else has ever and He suffered all of that at the hands of those He loved. The cross reminds us of the greatest suffering and the fullest forgiveness. Nevertheless, Jesus says, "Not my will, but thine, be done." Jesus knew His Father had a plan. That plan brought about a greater victory than any pain He would suffer.

I can't say that I understand why God let my daughter die or why it came to a point that we had to decide what to do with her life, literally. I can't say I understand the reason why her twin brother is now nearly four years old and can not talk or walk, can

59

not crawl or feed himself nor can he sit completely un-assisted by himself. Why did he have the stroke and now seizures? Why was he born with Down Syndrome? Why did we have two special needs children born on the same day and both needing an open-heart surgery? Why did our other children have to let go of a sister they loved so much and why did their little hearts have to be broken so deeply? Why did our twins, Grace and Gauge, have to suffer physically? Why did Grace die? I can't say I understand or that I hold the complete answers to all these things, but I can say when I remember the cross and what Christ did for me there, my own sufferings seem so small.

When I pay attention to the details of my life and what God has given me, I seem to find greater understanding. I remember the first time Grace smiled at me, the first time she opened her eyes and I knew she saw me, her mother, the familiar voice who now —— had a face. I remember holding her close to me to bring her comfort and how good that felt to me in bringing her that comfort! And, —— I remember her passing —— peacefully in my arms.

When I remember the cross, it is then that I live by faith. It is then that I can give thanks in **every single thing**! It is then that I learn to trust His Will.

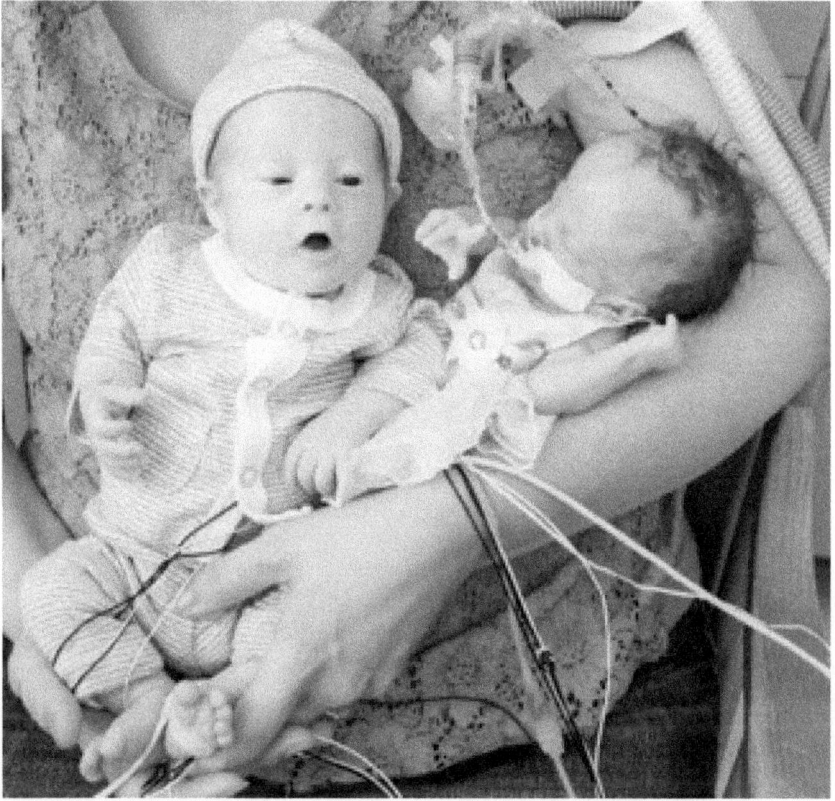

Our Twins, Gauge and Grace.

"IN EVERY THING GIVE THANKS; FOR <u>THIS</u> IS THE WILL OF

GOD IN CHRIST JESUS CONCERNING YOU."

I Thessalonians 5:18

CHAPTER 5

LIVING, WHILE WATCHING HER DIE

It was suffering on an uncharted scale! I was watching my baby die! Each time I walked over to her bedside, I felt an enormous weight come over me. I felt a dark cloud looming over my body and hers. It was death. It was there. It was waiting. I would take a deep sigh and then look at her and think, "If today is her last day, I've got to make it count!" I wanted her to experience me as a mother. I wanted to give her all I could in whatever time I was to be given with her. That meant I had to somehow live while watching her die.

I couldn't take her home, I couldn't breastfeed or even hold her whenever I wanted, for as long as I wanted. She was in critical care. She was on the brink of death, literally. I had a desire to give her all I could even though so many things couldn't and would never be experienced. I still had an overwhelming desire to somehow show my love to her. To be able to <u>mother</u> her in every way that I could.

Yes, there were boundaries I couldn't cross without potentially causing harm or even death. However, my love had no boundaries! I quickly learned to overcome the obstacle of filtering my pain so I could then express my love for her the way I so desired. Being a blubbering mess, who only saw the pain, would have left us with a deeper wound of not enjoying my time with her. It would also have left her without hearing me sing and seeing me smile! My daughter deserved to hear the joy in my heart of having her in my life!

On the rare occasions she opened her eyes, I would force a smile for her! Oh, my heart was glad to see those teeny, dark eyes but inside I was crushed to know I may never see them again. Those precious, little eyes staring right at me! It was magical. It was miraculous. It required so much of her energy just to open them. Then to recognize that she was acknowledging the voice she was so familiar with. No matter the heart pain I was feeling, I had to give her momma's smile each and every time she opened them for me.

She was fighting for life! It was painful to watch such a precious, innocent, tiny baby fight to live! And, when she opened her eyes, I had to smile. Sometimes tears would pour down my face, but I forced that smile for her, anyway. She needed to see me smile but most of all she deserved to see me smile!

She was fighting for life and I was fighting to live while watching her die. For the first few days after her birth I was encouraged not to touch her! Her heart was so defective that just touching her could be harmful to her health. That was so difficult, but I wanted to do what was best for her. I wanted to comfort her by giving her mother's touch and I didn't want to bring any type of harm in doing so! Her heart was so defective that even a diaper change caused her blood oxygen to drop into the teens and single digits. It was a knock at death's door everyday. The nurse would turn her on her side or pick her up just in the slightest and her oxygen would drop each and every time, most of the time into the twenties and thirties, but far too many times in the single digits. Her heart couldn't tolerate the change of blood flow. She had three significant heart defects including a very large hole in the center of her heart (VSD) and severe Double Outlet Right Ventricle (DORV).

Though most of her days brushed with death, there were also "good" days. Those were the days she didn't have to be given extra breaths on the ventilator, or days she didn't reach the single digits on her oxygen. There were also days of greater hope! For example, she was able to go from the IV nutrition to formula and from formula to my milk. She received the feeds by the g-tube that had been surgically placed the day she was born. She responded to her feedings well by having wet and dirty diapers, and even gaining weight. But, she did have a lethal chromosome defect. I frequently reminded myself of that fact to stay in reality mode.

On Mother's Day we almost lost her and the nurse told us that it wouldn't be a good day to hold her. Having her needs always in my best interest, I didn't hold her that day. I was thankful that most days, I could. I do remember asking God, "Why, on Mother's Day? Couldn't it have been another day?" Sure, it could have, and, possibly, I will never know the reason, but my only Mother's Day with Grace I was unable to hold her.

Instead of dwelling on things I didn't have, I would place my focus on things that I did have. This mindset got me through many tragic days! I was thankful she was alive. I was thankful that on that particular Mother's Day I didn't visit the graveside of my child. I was thankful to have that time with a child who statistically shouldn't have made it through birth. She had beaten so many odds already and her life everyday was a miracle!

I have a strong faith and I believe in God. I believe in miracles and I asked God to heal her *many times*! In faith, I believe He did, the second she arrived in Heaven! He did answer my prayers though not the way I had hoped! I asked for healing and God did INDEED heal her. She's dancing in heaven at this very moment and no longer struggles to breath. Her heart no longer looks as though it will pound straight out of her chest! She's quite well, now. She has been healed and she dine's with the KING!!!

My faith in God did make it easier to let her go, but getting to that place of acceptance took time. Time to process the reality that she was indeed going to die, and then time to apply my love through faith to that reality. Love enough to let her go and love enough to allow her to stop fighting to live. Love enough to take her off of life support twenty-four hours after we were told that her heart could never be repaired.

I had always maintained hope that she would live. I never lost that hope. I simply got to a place where I accepted reality and lived by that reality. Then, I hoped for her *living* to be where it was intended to be, in Heaven. I had my own ideas of what I wanted reality to actually be, but that was a make-believe world and I chose to also not *live* there.

I think the first time I saw her, I realized what a miracle she was. Seeing her for the first time literally took my breath away and it was one of those traumatic experiences that felt like an *out-of-body* experience. I was standing there looking at her fragile body while taking it all in. She was drenched with wires, on a ventilator and had a cut that covered nearly half of her tiny belly from the g-tube placement surgery given the day she was born. Her skin was so thin that I could see many of her veins. I was able to see her heart pounding away in her chest like it was going to jump out! Her little heart was working so hard! I stood there for an unknown period of time. I'm sure the look of both joy and fear crossed my countenance. It felt like I wasn't actually there, like I was in a dream and that it wasn't real. I even had difficulty recognizing that she was my own child. It briefly crossed my mind, "Is this really my daughter?" It seemed that she was not even from this world like an alien who belonged somewhere else. All of her medical needs made it look as though she wasn't even human. But the second I touched her, I knew this was my baby girl! The tears began to flow as I had just taken observation of her state.

A really good day was when I could hold her without her turning purple (nearly dying) just to be placed into my arms. In the beginning (at some point) I had to get over a fear of holding her. Unless you've lived it, you can't quite imagine what it's like to hold your child and face their death while doing it. You have to get the courage to look death in the face and say, "You won't keep me from giving this to her!" I was hoping she wouldn't die just because I held her. I was hoping she wouldn't suffer there in my arms while gasping for her lasts breaths.

I placed my trust and hope in The Lord. I trusted that whatever moment she were to die, it was going to be the way God allowed. It was going to be according to His plan. I trusted Him. My hope was in Him.

Modern medicine was used to keep her here, but modern medicine couldn't heal or fix her nor could anyone tell us exactly when or how she would die. No one knew, except God. I hoped in Him. I began asking Him for specific things regarding her health, but I trusted what He chose because my hope was in Him. My trust was in Him. My faith **is** in Him!

Seeing your child in that condition is a dagger to the heart like no one can possibly understand unless they have lived it themselves. For a parent in this situation it is a place of complete hopelessness that experiences places of complete desperation! Only my faith in God kept me sane!

For sixty-one days I walked into the NICU, got checked in, headed to the hand-washing area, scrubbed my hands, put on my gown and began to take my steps to see my critically ill child. I would feel a heaviness come over me that made it physically hard to walk and difficult to breath. I took shorter breaths. I felt my heart pounding. Anxious! I would become light-headed and at times would hear a ringing in my ears as though I was going to pass-out from the emotional heaviness causing me those physical symptoms.

I forced myself to think of the good, but before thinking on the good things, many thoughts of the grim reality would cross my mind. I would first think, "Will today be the day she dies? What is going to happen, today? If she dies, how painful will it be? How will she die?" These thoughts were my reality. I was "mom" to a terminally ill child. It was a real-life Hell on earth. How do you live? How do you live while watching your child die? How do you survive that kind of anguish? For me, that answer was to lean on the One, the only One, Who can get us through, anything!

Live by faith.

Faith in God helped me to look for the good. "Now faith is the substance of things hoped for, the evidence of things not seen." -Hebrews 11:1. Hoping in the good eased my heartache by thinking on the blessings. Hoping for those things which are not seen, our eternal home in heaven with our Lord Jesus, someday. Instead of thinking about her leaving this earth ——-

70

—— I thought about the day that I would see her again. With faith, I hoped for the things which were unseen.

I needed to think on good things because so many things were very wrong. You can't dwell on the heartbreak and not fall apart! So, you **must** find *life* in that moment. Find purpose. When I say, *"life"*, **I mean** the blessings of life *because of* **those things which are not seen.** God was a blessing to me. Jesus, in love, had given me everything I needed to go to heaven and be with my little girl one day. God had given me this beautiful life, Grace's life. I was blessed to be her mother! These were some of the good things that I thought about.

Faith causes you to see the blessings and trust a plan that you can not see.

I personally had a desire to make the best of all things, even those gut-wrenching one's. So, instead of screaming and crying (like I wanted to so many times), I would hold it together for her, for them ——- for my family. Reasonably, I understood that having an emotional breakdown wasn't going to save her life; that wasn't going to get the answers that I wanted. My out-pouring of emotions could not change her physical state. However, I could help the situation by being reasonable in my

71

response to the pain I was feeling. A reasonable response at times such as these is only found through love. Love motivated me to make a hellish situation as pleasant as I possibly could for everyone. Because that's what mom's do, or at least, what they should do. Faith in God prompted me to such a love.

No amount of money can change a terminal diagnosis. No verbal demand I could make would make my sick child, well. No amount of drugs or alcohol can diminish the pain of watching this; it could only mask a wound that will be there day after day. The end result would be greater problems by turning to those things during such times of great, emotional vulnerability and distressing heart pain.

Many will drink and do drugs to excessive amounts. They are attempting to mend a wound that is extremely deep so it will take large amounts of *something* to mask it. **If you don't give this big burden over to God, you will find yourself in a big mess.** A mess you weren't equipped to handle. Remember death was never in God's original plan, so when He created mankind, we were not equipped to handle death. Only God has the capability of mending a wound that large!

Trusting God gave me the hope to cope. He is still the source on which I lean.

72

"For my thoughts are not your thoughts, neither are your ways my ways, saith the Lord. For as the heavens are higher than the earth, so are my ways higher than your ways, and my thoughts than your thoughts." -Isaiah 55:8-9 God's ways aren't the same as mine. I had the choice to trust His ways or lean unto my own thoughts. By choice: I simply recognized and yielded to the God Who created her life. He could heal her, but should He choose not to, I trusted His plan. He is perfect. I am not! He spoke daylight and darkness into existence. He spoke the life of each creature on land, sea and air. "And the Lord God formed man of the dust of the ground, and breathed into his nostrils the breath of life; and man became a living soul." Genesis 2:7

Now that, dear folks, ——- is **perfection!**

Faith in a real God and His real heaven! <u>Heaven is for real!</u>

I believe my little girl is in heaven. I believe she can come and go at the feet of Jesus Christ. I believe that for all eternity she will no longer experience illness or death. I believe she walks streets of gold and shares a heavenly home with other loved ones. I believe God. I trust His ways. I have faith in Him because of His love for me. This real faith has gotten me

73

through a real, dark time and it continues to bring the hope in seeing my little Grace again, one day.

He is God. I know He loves me. I know He loves Grace. Knowing this caused me to trust His ways. It was then that I was able to live by faith and be thankful for what I was given. The moments I was given. The defining acts of love that took place through her life because He made her mine! Those beautiful things I had been given through her life, the life of my daughter, Grace.

Had I only focused on her illness, I would have missed out on the blessings. If I couldn't see past her physical distress, I couldn't have seen what a joy she was to have in my life; even if it was only sixty-one days. She was a new person and she is an eternal being created by God. Her beginning has no end. She will live forever and —— her forever is with the Lord!

My love through faith was enough to see beyond the bad and focus on the good awaiting my little Grace. That love was given to me by God. It gave me the ability to do what was best for my daughter and for my family; thinking of them and not myself. Bringing comfort to them while I was being crushed, and singing to Grace and Gauge though I struggled in fear of their conditions. It was the love that God had given me allowing me to access the faith needed to *live* while watching her die.

CHAPTER 6

THE CLOTHES SHE NEVER WORE

Early this week I was contacted by an acquaintance of mine asking if anyone had some items to give to a young couple about to welcome their new baby girl. I immediately thought of some clothes that were bought for Grace, clothes she never wore. (I had all the clothes she did wear tucked away in a tote.) Now the clothes that she had not worn were either going to continue sitting in the basket they were in or become someone else's. That day, I chose to sort through them and give them away.

While going through the clothes, I felt very empty. It felt as if there was no-one else in the world at that moment, except me. Like the whole earth was empty of people. I moved slowly through those clothes, almost afraid to grab something that could uncover more tragedy. As if I would pickup another garment that would reveal more loss or that I was going to lose another part of me; reaching a new level of grief that I hadn't yet experienced.

These were the clothes she never wore and never would wear.

It was so quiet and lonely sitting there going through them; I couldn't even hear myself breath. It was like I was deaf for a time. If my children were being noisy in another part of the house that day, I didn't hear them. I experienced complete silence and felt so alone.

I fought the tears for as long as I could while sorting through the clothes to give away, but when the tears came my face felt cold and the tears very warm. I breathed heavy breaths. Everything was still and seemingly ———— calm. I felt that what I was doing was something monumental. At the time it seemed like I was having an appointed meeting with my own life. An appointment that no one but me was aware of.

I was in the process of making one of the most important decisions concerning my future and it's outcome and I was doing it alone. My future and its dance with grief was being formulated. As if I was cutting the pattern to my *dress*. This was the monumental decision being made for the outcome of my life beyond grief. What the *dress* was going to look like when it was finished. What I was doing at that moment was either going to leap me forward in healing or leave me bitter and broken. Was I going to find healing or stay bound by grief?

76

Is there ever a *good* time to go through your deceased child's clothes? Does it ever feel okay to give them away? As a parent we naturally ask the questions, "Why am I having to do this, anyway? Why did my child die?" These questions are natural but can impose a great danger as this loss has reached a depth like no other. The danger in asking this question is that we will likely never get the answer and because we likely will not have an answer, it is easy to become bitter in the lack of an answer. This will probably be the greatest hurt we will ever experience in our lifetime. We have been victimized by death and not just any death, the death of our child.

The greater the hurt, the greater potential to become bitter.

Bitterness robs us of every joy life brings. Bitterness will choke us of all good things; twenty-four hours a day and seven days a week. It will take all *life* out of living. If bitterness was a weed in the garden of life, it officially takes over everything gorgeous in your garden. God says it like this in Hebrews 12:15b, "...lest any root of bitterness springing up trouble you..."

Relationships are broken when you become bitter because you hate the world and everyone in it! That's what bitterness does! Your life is snuffed-out by this evil source, brought about by a hurt you've faced that you just couldn't seem to get over. It was just too large of a hurt! Your child is gone! Your child died! It is so easy to become bitter!

During that moment of going through her clothes, I was given a choice. God gave me the ability to choose how I would live. In life each day I am faced with choices. *It is my responses to the stormy seasons of life that formulate the path to where my future will be once the storm is over.* In that time of what seemed to be a *Hell on earth*, I had a choice that changed everything about my future! I could dwell on the loss and live in that *Hell* in which I had no control (become bitter), or I could get some healing in the grieving process by giving her clothes to someone else (become better).

I did have control over how I grieved. I could go through her clothes and angrily throw them screaming, "It's not fair! She should be here! God, why did you let my baby die?" OR, I could find some outfits to give to a family in need of clothes for their soon to be baby girl. I could also have left them to sit and only exist in my world as if they were dust on my selfish table of grief. Decisions, decisions, choices, choices ——— I had them.

To grieve and die or heal and live.

78

As I made my decision that day to give some of those clothes away, I recall thinking, "Grace's clothes in heaven are so much nicer than these." I also recall mentally recognizing (and I may have even spoken these embedded words out loud), "So this is what they feel ———— what they go through ————— mother's who've lost their children ———— this is what it feels like to go through their clothes." There was a long and quiet pause as I sat there just looking at the piles of clothes that I had gone through. This is the point when the tears came. I just stared and sat there with that same heaviness, only then ———— I didn't feel so lonely. In a strange sort of way, I didn't just grieve Grace that day; I also grieved the loss of every child whose mother had also quietly and painfully sat while sorting through their clothing. I could almost hear each mother's moaning cry as, I too, knew it well. I no longer felt alone that day.

I don't have the answer as to why a particular parent buries a child while another doesn't. I do know that had I personally never experienced the death of my child, I couldn't write about it, today. This book exist because of another grieving mother from Indiana; a mother who buried her daughter in a graveyard just three miles from her home. Her daughter's gravestone is engraved with a name of one she will never forget. Not a single day will she, or, can she, forget. That grave contains the

79

remains of the body of a small and beautiful, baby girl. My baby girl. This book exist because a mother, by the Grace of God, found the faith and courage to let her baby go; receiving the inspiration and clarity of mind to write about it. This book exist because the God of Heaven and earth gave this mother (who just so happens to be me) the faith needed to know her daughter's life continues in Heaven, in our hearts AND in the clothes she never wore.

CHAPTER 7

DEAR, GRIEVING MOTHER
(my letter to you)

Dear Mother,

As I sit here to write this letter to you all, tears began to flood my eyes just as I typed in the title of this chapter. My throat has that burning sensation you get when you are holding back the tears. The screen of my laptop is difficult to see now because my eyes are full of your heartbreak. My eyes are full of your tears and they are streaming down as I type. The pain is so very real; I know that pain! I ask God, "What should I say to them? I know what I wish to accomplish with this letter, but what do I say in order to do that? GOD, HELP ME!"

If I told you that I understood everything you've gone through, that couldn't be further from the truth. We have all faced a different path that led each of us to this place of **deep sorrow**. I have learned that so much of our grief goes unspoken. I think that is because many of us have a difficult time putting into words what we feel. Through the writings of this book I believe much of that is revealed and I have found a lot of this to be universal between us.

My daughter's body lies in a coffin of a cemetery located three miles from my home. I personally placed her dead body in the arms of the nurse who had cared for her much of her life; this was the last time I held her. A friend of mine, who is also a funeral home director, came to pick up her body from the hospital that day. He told me that as he drove her to the funeral home (an hour away from the hospital), he kept her in the seat next to him wrapped in the blanket I held her in when she died. I was later given the blanket in a bag of things the funeral home had kept for us once the services were over.

In my home, in a small tote, is every physical memory I possess of my little Grace. Some items in that tote include a locket of her hair, some of her clothing, her blankets, pictures and even the copies of the letters my other children had written and placed in her casket. I have memories, but I don't have Grace.

I try my best to remember what it felt like to have her in my arms as I bury my face in her fabrics each time while going through the tote. I sniff desperately for her scent and then escape for a moment with a smile on my face as I imagine her back in my arms again. I find my arms and hands in the position of a mother lovingly holding her child and then, too soon, reality sets in; I realize my arms are empty. I remember again that she isn't here anymore. I cry silently, again. Not everyone needs to know how hard this is and there's no possible way they could understand it unless they too, have lived it.

What I do know about you, dear mother, is what it is like to have this loss. I don't know how much you miss your child, but I do know how much you have lost. I know that eerie, moaning cry of grief in the death of a child; a cry like I have not experienced before that day, had never heard before and (thank God) have not heard since.

The day after Grace died, I cried all day. To this day, it is still known as my day of deep and dark grief. Though my grieving has been deep and dark through its entirety ———- that day was different; I stayed in a state of *emptiness*. It was a part of me that I had never known before. It was as if *something* took over my body and *owned* it, possessed it. It seemed as if I had no control over my crying. I moaned an eerie cry all day. This cry became absent of tears and the best I can describe it was that <u>the grief possessed my body.</u> It was me grieving, yet, it wasn't me. It really felt like *it* controlled me.

83

Dear Mother, I understand the void you feel everyday being consciously aware that a part of you is missing from this earth. I comprehend the *fog* you live in each day as you **try** to function *normal* again. I remember desperately seeking out the reason for all of this. I thought that surely something this tragic must have a significant reason we faced this. Much of my focus in the beginning was spent on looking to find that reason. I wasted a lot of time looking.

Truth is, it likely isn't meant for us to _know_ the reason but only rather to _trust_ the reason. We are to trust God in His plan and believe with all of our hearts that He has a purpose for all of this. That He has a reason why we are grieving mothers. Many of you are cussing me right now. That's okay, really. I'm no stranger to anger, or fear, or hurt, or pain nor am I a stranger to grief. Your potential anger with me I realize would be misdirected. I know Who (God) you are really angry with. I've been angry with Him, too, and somedays I am still angry.

Trusting God doesn't mean that you will do everything right. You can't do everything one-hundred percent right (you are human.) Now, take a deep breath (literally) and release the air slowly. Do this several times. Is it quiet? You need it quiet right now. Then (out loud) tell yourself, "I'm going to make some mistakes in all of this grieving stuff. I am hurt. I'm very hurt and

I'm going to make some mistakes in my grief." Cause you see, momma, it's hard to bandage a bleeding wound. Bandages won't stick to wet skin. You've got a long way to go to get the bleeding to stop. You are injured and most likely you are *bleeding* more than you ever will in your entire life, so you are going to make some mistakes. It's going to take a bit of time to get some healing and find the right *bandage* for the job.

Scripture tells us in the book of Job that when Job found out all ten of his children were killed and that he had also lost all of his fortune in a single day, "In all this Job sinned not, nor charged God foolishly." - Job 1:22. Here in Scripture we learn of a man who lost more than we ever will and didn't sin or blame God while going through it. (We are not going to compare ourselves to Job because he was an exceptional human being. God leaves his testimony for each of us in His Eternal Word as an example of how to live as Christian's through terrible tragedies.) Job's testimony was so amazing, it was inspired by God and written in His Word for us to read about thousands of years later in the most published book of all time, The Holy Bible. If there were a bunch of *Jobs* back then, the Bible would be full of stories like his, but there simply weren't a bunch of Jobs then or now. However, through his example we are compelled to trust God and live perfectly.

85

Grief brings a great depth of emotion with it! With that deep and unforgiving emotion comes *vulnerability*. You are quite vulnerable and have now entered a **classroom** of life like no other. *You will learn more about yourself than you likely ever will through any other season of life, past or future!* This classroom, for a grieving mother, is like no other! It is the classroom from the burning pits of *Hell* entwined with the grace from the heights of **Heaven**.

If we envisioned this room, we could see ourselves sitting at a desk. In the front of the classroom is God Almighty. He can not be removed from His position as Teacher of the class, though Satan is also completely visible in the room. He is the tempter; the distraction (if you will) that is present in the room along with God and ourselves. Satan has had permission to enter the classroom where we are the only student.

It is as though we are completely naked and alone with God and Satan in this classroom. There is nothing preventing the greatest harm towards us by the claws of Satan himself. At the same time there is nothing preventing us from the deliverance of God. We are vulnerable, we are exposed, and have been ripped-up by Satan in the death of our child. And we are completely capable of receiving a healing calm through God the Instructor. Both God and Satan are easily accessible.

Now, we are naked to every degree possible. What we knew of ourselves before entering this room on this day is only a memory. Nothing about who we were before is going to be the same. We will be different in every way. Once this lesson has been taught, we will walk out with the greatest strength and healing that will ever take place in our lives **OR** we will crawl out bleeding and struggling to take our next breath. This is what **will** happen; one of the two.

During the course of the lesson we will have been stripped of any and all *masks* we may have knowingly or unknowingly carried in life with us. Any strength of our own accord will be destroyed. It will be ripped off! *No more masks.* To this depth of nakedness, nothing remains. We are stripped of everything and Satan has danced with us in death and grief leaving us bound in chains of wounds like we have never seen.

The Teacher sits quietly in the front of the room, instructing—
—— lovingly and quietly, instructing. Compassion beholds Him. Peace adorns Him. Love radiates from Him, to Him and in Him! Tears flood the Teacher's eyes and pain grieves His own heart. He knows what suffering we face in our grief. He too, has buried a Child. A Perfect Child. A Blameless Child. A Loving Child. The Teacher is no stranger to this bloody battle of grief. He knows it well. He understands it fully. The cuts and battle scars

at Satan's hand are imprinted on His Own Heart. He too, has experienced the sorrow! Scripture says for three days God turned His back on the earth when Christ died. God Himself couldn't face it! DARKNESS covered the universe for those three entire days that God had His back turned; there was no light on the earth for three days.

Just when you think that no one understands, you realize that even He understands. The Teacher was once a Student. Scripture says that nothing we will face is uncommon to Him. He knows every sorrow and every pain! "There hath no temptation taken you but such as is common to man..." - I Corinthians 10:13a.

Jesus was once the Student. Jesus is God. Jesus lived on this earth for thirty-three years as a man. He faced every temptation that we have faced. God also faced the death of His Son, Jesus. You may ask, "How is Jesus —— God and also The Son of God?" The easiest way to describe the answer to that question is this: If you took an egg and separated it into three different parts, (shell, yolk and white) you still end up having the same egg only separated into the three parts. The Father, Son and Holy Ghosts are all One in the same. So we can then say that Jesus and God are The Teacher and have been The Student.

All we must do, now, as the student, is simply look towards the front of the room and acknowledge Him (the Teacher and one time Student.) Sometimes in the fight all we can do is look toward the front of the classroom. Not even the words, "God, help me!" can be uttered. We are that weak ——- that low ——- that hurt —— that wounded —— that exposed ——- that naked —— that vulnerable ——- that broken ——- bound by grief and bleeding uncontrollably. Satan's fierce attack is relentless.

But if God is good enough for us to trust in His eternal Heavenly home (that our child now rests in), why wouldn't He be good enough to trust in the process of how we all get there (assuming you are going there?) Do you believe Heaven is a real and perfect place? Do you believe your child is there? How then could there be a perfect, eternal home (Heaven) that safely houses our children ——- without a perfectly, wonderful God? There would be no paradise without the Creator of the paradise. There would have not been anyone to love our child without the Father of all Love! The Teacher! The Instructor! The Student! GOD ——- JESUS CHRIST!

One day we hope, in faith, to join our child in Heaven along with God the Father and God the Son. Until then, dear mother, trust Him for when that time will be. Heaven was ready for your child, but it's not yet ready for you. (You understand me, don't

89

you?) Trust our perfect God Who created the perfect Heaven your child lives in with the perfect timing of when you will join them!

Faith will bring the hope you need to wait and the endurance you need to sustain the pain of waiting. (Read that again.)

While you wait, think of this: there is no *time* in Heaven. Your child isn't sitting around waiting on you. The truth is, they aren't even missing you ——- at all! There is no sadness in Heaven. In fact, if we could make a phone call to Heaven today and ask God to put your child on the phone, do you know what they would say? They would say something like this, "Mom, you should see this place! You wouldn't believe how beautiful it is and how big it is! I'm not sick anymore, mom, and I feel awesome! I don't hurt a bit and I'm never sad or lonely! I can run or fly or jump or walk whenever I want to and as much as I want! I have lots of friends here too, more than I ever had down there. I play with Jesus everyday and He is awesome at everything! There isn't anything He can't do! He has taught me so much and I love to just hear Him talk. His voice is so familiar and He says a lot of smart things. And Mom, please stop crying all the time. I don't get sad here but I see how sad you are all the time. If you knew how good I had it, you wouldn't cry so much for me. It was my time to go because my life was complete. Everything He created me to do and to be was finished. Please be sure you make it here too, because I've seen the place God has ready for you here and it is SO AWESOME! Tell everyone that I'm doing great and tell them to get here, too! I will see you when it's time. Don't worry about me. I want you to be happy! You have lots of reasons to keep living and lots of things left for you to do! I have to go now, Mom. It's time for me to sing, oh yeah, I forgot to tell you that I sing in this huge, angel choir up here and it is like nothing you have ever heard before! I will sing for you when you get here. Talk to you later. Love you, Mom! -bye-" I'm pretty sure that's about what they would say only with the excitement and enthusiasm a child in Heaven could exclaim! (Is it possible that your child asked God to send this book to you in order to find healing?)

Mothers with children in Heaven, I do know how hard it is to live with that deep absence. The living of each day with someone, so dear, missing. To never live one day again without the knowledge of their absence. The void that seems to always be present. I've felt the tingling sensation in my toes and fingertips with that surge of energy that comes over you when you feel your emotions are coming *unglued.* I'm pretty sure that

91

energy literally comes from the pits of Hell through Satan himself. I know what it feels like when you think you are just about to lose your *ever-livin'-mind* and then you somehow pull yourself together, take a deep breath and move forward. Well, maybe you move backwards or sideways, but you move. You function. You exist.

I know what it's like to function in that foggy state of mind. You can't even remember where you slept last night. Did you sleep? You aren't even sure. Did you eat? You can't concentrate long enough to answer. Then someone says, "God won't give you anything you can't handle" and you just feel like screaming or choking them! You think to yourself, "They wouldn't say that if they were me!"

The truth is, God is there when we fall apart. He wants to be the shoulder we lean on. He simply doesn't give us anything we can't handle ——— without Him. Key words, "without Him" because we are given plenty we **can not** handle on our own. The death of a child seems to top them all! People don't walk these steps we have taken and make it through alive without a real God above tending to them while they are in this classroom.

I want you all to know that when you feel like you are alone, you aren't. When you think no one cares, Someone does. When you fear how death will happen to your child (if you haven't already lived it) there is someone else who does know what that fear is like; what that pain is like. I do, and I say with assurance that **with God** ———- you will survive it. With Him, you will make it through this! I hope and pray that you walk out healed and comforted! God forbid you crawl out broken and bleeding! God Forbid!

No matter where you are on this journey, my advice to you all is to live and love as much as you can each day. Smile for your dying child. Laugh with your living children. Watch a movie. Do something normal. Play a game. Take walks outside breathing in deep sniffs of the air while listening for birds to sing to you. Talk to God. Vent to Him. He can handle it. Stand outside at night during a snow-fall and relish in the serenity. Have a picnic in the springtime when the flowers are beginning to bloom. Make love to your spouse. Give someone a gift just because. Make treat bags for your children. Clean your house and freshen the smell of the air with your favorite scent. LIVE.

Look for God in every detail of your life, YOU WILL FIND HIM evident in every aspect of every part of your day ——- if you look. Tell God what your favorite color is and ask Him to let you see it. Tell Him what your favorite shape or animal is (He already knows but make it known to Him that you want Him to be that specific with you) and ask Him to show it to you throughout your day. See what He does for you. Ask Him for a vacation day or some type of reprieve. Talk to Him. Depend on Him. Ask Him to help you. Count on Him because He will be there, always! Most of all, yield yourself to Him. You will learn to trust Him even when the answer you want doesn't come.

You were chosen by God for probably the most difficult task a woman could live through. I say, "chosen," because God was very aware it was going to happen. He allowed it to happen. He could have stopped it, but He didn't.

God only knows where you will journey on this path of grief. He knows **if** or **when** you will shut Him out of your life. He will wait on you. Believe it or not, He truly loves you! He never joyed to see you or your child suffer. He does desire to see the victory that He knows you can have! Remember that He sees the things that we can not see! God knows what a catapult of power you will gain in the strength He can give you if you trust Him with your whole heart. Do you know what God did for Job? He gave Job double what he had originally owned AND He gave him ten MORE children!

God has a plan. A beautiful plan. Trust Him with the plan He has for your life and see what will happen. I did and I wrote this book. A book He knew I would write and a book He knew that you would read, —— long before I first laid eyes on my little

94

Grace and long before I let her go, ——- He knew you were going to read this! Don't limit God and what He can do in your classroom. Just look to the front of the class and acknowledge the Teacher. You will walk out comforted and fit to take on the world!

With Deepest Sympathy,

~Heather

CHAPTER 8

LOVE, FROM HEAVEN

The day we buried our two month old daughter, Amazing Grace, (while in transport from the service to the graveside) I rode in the back of the limousine with her twin brother on my lap and three of our five other children. I had a window seat. My husband was escorted to the front passenger seat and our two other children rode together in the seat between my husband and I. The sky was perfectly clear and very blue that day. It was a sunny, Sunday afternoon and a beautiful one at that!

While gazing up into the sky and thanking God for giving me the strength to endure such a day, a large blue heart in the sky caught my attention. It was white clouds shaped into a perfect heart and the center of it was the vibrant blue sky! I immediately told the Lord, "Thank you, I love you, too!" I knew that something so perfect sitting up there in the sky at just the right angle for me to see it was purposefully done, so I thanked God for doing it and responded quietly, but verbally.

We made the turn onto a different highway and a mile or so down, another heart! This one was all white, for it was clouds shaped into a heart with a tag on the bottom connecting to another larger group of clouds. I shed a few tears at this point and said, "God, you are just awesome! Thank You!" I knew those heart-shaped clouds were for me!

We arrived at the graveside. Service was as solemn as one could imagine. I knew I would see her again. I had peace. It was a gorgeous day to lay her body at rest.

Her twin brother sat on the lap of my husband during the graveside service. Once it was finished, the funeral director began handing out the roses from her spray. He started with me, then my husband, then each of our children, grandmothers and aunts but the rose that was given to my husband for her twin brother immediately started to shed its petals. We loaded back into the limousine and realized what had just happened. With just half of the rose in hand, we asked that the petals that had fallen from her twin brother's rose be picked up and placed on her casket. It was unbelievable! None of the other roses shed petals and there is no other explanation than to understand the bond of twins. It was a beautiful ending ceremony to her beautiful life!

I woke up very early the next morning; it was still dark out. I wanted to see the sun come up that first morning from her graveside, so I made my way down to the cemetery. I sat on my knees next to her grave and looked toward the eastern skies. It was a cloudy morning. I could see where the sun was beginning to come up but I couldn't actually see it until it popped through the leaves of a tree. This was no ordinary tree. It was a tree that had been stripped of every branch except a few on top from a tornado that had come through just over a year before. It was a tall, mature tree. It's branches and leaves that remained, formed a perfect heart at the top! It had this very large and bare trunk and then at its top (about 60-70 ft.) was an arrangement of branches and leaves remaining to form a perfect heart-shape. I know my mouth must have dropped open and I couldn't tell you how long I sat there and stared, crying with joy! I was being loved from Heaven by God and I knew it without a single doubt!

Before I left that morning I went to kneel and pray. As I placed my right hand on the ground, just in-between my thumb and index-finger, another heart in the grass! It was a type of leafy grass that was shaped as a perfect heart! It was indeed a great love being shared with me from Heaven! I didn't deserve it or earn it, but I was given it! Ironically the definition of **"grace"**

is unmerited favor of God. Finding favor in God's sight without doing anything to earn it! Amazing Grace! Love, From Heaven.

On the way home that morning, after spending several hours at the cemetery, I began to cry amazing tears of joy! I recalled the day our daughter died. She was within minutes of passing on and she was placed in my arms wrapped in a hand-made pink afghan that had been donated to the hospital. I recalled that hearts were sewn-in all over it! When I made the connection of all those events I was overwhelmed with joy!!! The heart afghan, the heart clouds, the heart tree and grass were all signs from God to me. He was sending His love and He knew I would notice! Love, From Heaven.

This morning my friend, Vonda, messaged me telling me that she asks God for reminders to pray for me. She said while baking a cake last week she noticed a perfect heart in the center of the cake. I replied back to my friend and told her that last week one of our son's therapist didn't know my "heart" story and she brought a teething ring for him that had a heart on it! The next day, one of the other therapist (who did know the story), said that two days after I told her the story about the hearts, she was making jewelry when two of the small metal pieces fell together on the table forming a perfect heart! She brought those pieces that day to show me! She was so amazed by it that she couldn't wait to share the story with me! We were being loved from Heaven!

So, why am I prompted to share this today? Immediately after reading the text from my friend this morning about the cake, I walked out to check my garden and glanced down at some landscaping rocks. Amidst all the other black stones ———- I see this one heart-shaped rock! It popped out at me! I picked it up, set it on the pavement and took a picture of it while telling God that I loved Him, too! He is amazing! He is big! He is too big to be overlooked! Give Him a chance to show you His love! The definition of Grace is "unmerited favor of God." Wow! We don't deserve it and we can't earn it but He gives it! **LOVE, From Heaven.** I hope you will now begin or continue to notice it!

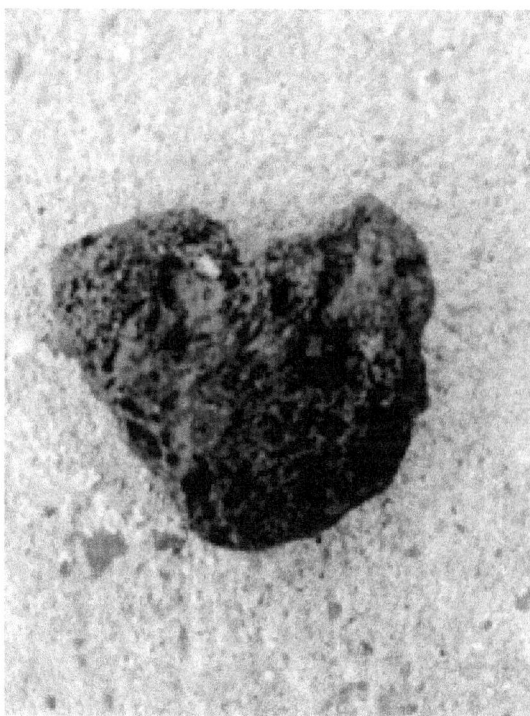

CHAPTER 9

UNDERSTANDING A GRIEVING FATHER

Commonly men are known as "Mr. Fix-it." A title earned (no doubt) by their repair skills around the house both indoor and out. Sometimes the women of the common households find difficulty replacing certain light bulbs and heaven help us if an entire light fixture is in need of replacement! That's a man's job. Right? Along with the heavy outdoor stuff and all those household gadgets that are much too complex, but we can read the mind's of our husband's before they speak, catch a dish mid-air before if crashes to the floor while on the phone scheduling an appointment because we "saw that one coming!" But gadgets and gizmos are guy stuff! What is foreign territory for most of the ladies, we leave those things for dear 'ol, Mr. Fix-it, Dad.

It's a running joke at my house (when some heavier duties inside or outside are needing to be done) for me to explain to my husband that, "You have hide (as in cowhide) and I have skin!" Though I don't have to plead my case to get his help, I find humor in reminding him of how tough his skin is verses mine. Sometimes he asks me "Make a fist," just so he can laugh at my tiny, little fists verses his own Wreck-It Ralph fists.

Men and women, we have our differences that make us unique in our families. Mothers have those unique voices that can be used to soothe a crying baby but can you imagine what it would sound like to hear Morgan Freeman sing your baby a lullaby? You would likely have a screaming, crying baby! Seriously though! My husband is great at putting together the crib with its nuts, bolts and washers, BUT he has been the least successful placing sleeping babies in it.

Dad gets called in with the big jobs, the physically complicated ones or when things get really tough. It's good 'ol dad that is called in to be the problem solver, the fix-it guy! Momma wipes away the tears from her daughter's eyes when she gets her heart broken but daddy draws the line in the sand and says, "Cross it, Mr. Heartbreaker and see what happens to ya!" Strong and tough, the family hero, good ol' dad ——- our Mr. Fix-it.

But what happens to Mr. Fix-it when your child is diagnosed terminal, stricken with some debilitating disease or becomes completely disabled? What happens to him when your child dies? What happens to him when he can no longer be the hero of those complicated scenarios; when the job is too big and he can't fix it? What happens to him when all of that desire to remove the problems from the lives of those he loves most is crushed when the doc says, "I'm sorry, there's nothing we can do?" Then momma leans over to the shoulder of big and strong dad, cries a cry from the pits of Hell, looks to him in hope that he can do something (because he always has) but this time he can't.

Your child dies. Now what? Mr. Fix-it is now, Mr. Broken. He's broken and the problem can't be fixed by him, anyway. This is a problem beyond dad's solving. It is completely out of his reach and because he can always seem to find a fix to most every problem the family faces, this one ——- breaks him.

Dad thinks he is holding up for everyone but what he doesn't realize is that his "thinker" is broken. He thinks he is still in this fight as our heroic dad Mr. Fix-It, but he isn't. He is broken. Every dad that has a terminally ill child or has buried a child is broken and until he is fixed, he will be unaware of his frantic, irrational state.

Because dads are the *head Fred* of the house (or at least are supposed to be/you gotta have just one chief) he is the go-to-guy for problems. He carries this massive load everyday. It's hard for mothers to understand it, really. We just can't understand the pressure they are under in their desire to meet the needs of the family, all the while keeping up with some heavy responsibilities.

As a mother, I know what it's like to keep up with appointments, household chores, banking, insurance, sick children, well children, holidays, birthdays and all of those never-ending scheduling conflicts caused by practices and school activities, but I don't know what it's like to be the father who must provide for all of those and try to keep up with many of them. Providing and then protecting what he's providing for. Keeping up with his own set of chores and scheduling conflicts, then work and his family.

Think about it like this. If a family goes bankrupt, who do most people blame? It's dad. He is supposed to fill in the gaps and make sure that everything is accounted for. He is supposed to make the decisions of where and how the money is being spent and when it all goes south, so goes the way of the da-da bird, Dad. He's the one that faces the blame.

Dad will search for a fix for this deep and dark family problem! Frantically he will search and he may even grasp at straws by turning to alcohol, drugs, women, becoming a work-aholic, or a list of other things. He may never go to the right place for healing. He may never go to God for the fix. He may remain broken for the rest of his life. He may grasp at straws for the remainder of his days here on this earth. He may remain broken. He may or he may not.

You've heard the saying, "You can bring a horse to water but you can't make him drink;" the same can be said for each of us when it comes to times of despair and need. The help may be accessible but we don't have to take it. *The male ego can prolong the right help especially in a deeply, grieving man* ——— ——— Dads in particular. A grieving father is a broken man in need of repair; in need of a super-healing.

Many men will struggle to get this healing because of pride. Dad doesn't want to admit he is broken in the first place and if he does admit it, he certainly doesn't want to admit he needs to go elsewhere to get the help; being as he is so strong and tough. You know, male pride. You can't fault him completely; God made him to have those strong acts of valiant character. But at the same time, God made all of creation under Himself. He is God. We are not. God can do anything and everything. Men, women, we can not. So, dad can't quite fix everything, not this time.

Dad, (yes, I'm addressing you specifically) you can fight all you want to on this one; regretfully, *and I do hate to admit this,* but ——- you can't win. <u>It grieves my heart to say it!</u> It pains me just as much to know it. I, too, have faced this grief though I do understand that I'm not a man. I am a woman and I do know there is a difference. You see, I was made by God to be the *weaker vessel.* Men were made to be stronger physically and mentally, the stronger vessel. Leaders. So, I do understand that we are different, even in our grieving.

As a woman, I was made to be more tender by my softer touches and richer emotions. I was made to notice things my husband wouldn't and he was made to notice things I couldn't. Men are different in their stronger touches and drier emotions. The fellas are a bit more vague than we are. As a woman, I know that my emotions sit on my shoulder more often than my husband's do. I know that he is better at those big jobs, indoor and out. I go to him for the most complicated problems of the household with the gadgets and the people of our home. He's my physical go-to-guy for all the tough problems.

Those things being said, I admit that I'm the weaker of the two of us. I was made to be that way, and therefore, it is easier for me to submit or yield to something or someone. My husband, on the other hand, was made to lead our home. As a natural-born leader, it is tougher for him to yield. Do you see where I'm going with this? Dad, it is harder for you to put up your white flag of surrender in this horrendous battle of grief. You want to *take the bull by the horns* in this grieving thing and steer it where you want it to go. BUT YOU CAN'T. You will try. You will fight, but fighting in your own strength will bring more difficulties. You are going to run out of your own strength. Remember, this is something **you** can't fix, at least, not in your own strength. You can wrestle it all you want, but eventually you will tire. Your strength will fail because it is as if you are bound up completely in a trapper and you are fiercely tugging and pulling away from something you can't remove yourself from. The more you fight it, the more it takes hold of you.

The *why* this happened —— isn't for you to figure out. The *how* to fix it all ——- is not for you to fix. **<u>The blame</u>** for it belongs solely to Satan. The questions and venting you have, God can handle. And, as hard as it is, you have to let this go. This wasn't an attack toward you or your family by God; this was an attack toward your family by Satan. He's the usher of death. He is the reason mankind was tempted to sin, leading to each of our deaths, and Satan has a desire to tear your family apart through this loss! That desire reaches a height that you *could never* recognize. (I elaborate on this throughout other parts of this book.)

You can't heal your child or bring them back from death, but you can yield this decision over to God. You can realize that it was He who decided the when and how. Yes, Satan was the usher of death and desires for this to rip you in every way, but God allowed it to *cross His desk and gave it His stamp of approval.*

God can stop Satan. God can stop death. God can heal and when He doesn't do these things we are to trust the bigger picture. That trust comes through faith. That faith is activated by our yielding. Surely it would be easier if we could see that place called Heaven that our child now lives in, wouldn't it? It would be much easier.

This is where faith comes in. With faith, we can *see* those things which are not seen. It takes a surrendered man/woman holding up their little white flag towards heaven to activate this type of faith. I envision a couple with tear-filled eyes, hidden behind a small, dirt hill, peeping their heads up over it, flag in hand's, waving them back and forth as their heavy eyes look towards God above. Without saying so, because they are so beat down, they surrender to His Will. Unknowingly, they are now receiving the healing they long hoped for.

Surrender doesn't mean that we will no longer feel the pain of grief. Surrender means we no longer feel beat down

110

from the fight. This is something we can't beat; something we can't change and dad has a harder time getting to that place of surrender and trust. Faith will help dad and mom see the bigger picture. Faith will help us see God's plan for our child's life. Faith will help us see that our child has already lived-out their entire life's purpose. **Faith will help us see Heaven and get there to be with our child one, glad day!**

Understanding dad, means understanding how he was made. He likes being the hero. He loves to fix the family problems and he even enjoys being the strong shoulder (stronger vessel) to lean on. He wants to be valiant in this great battle his family has faced, he wants to be the family hero, but this is something he can't fix and suddenly his shoulders are not so big. That for him, is a hard pill to swallow.

Dad (I'm addressing you again), as I shared with the mothers reading this book, you just need to look toward the front of the _classroom_ and see your God! "The Lord is my rock, and my fortress, and my deliverer; my God, my strength, in whom I will trust; my buckler, and the horn of my salvation, and my high tower. I will call upon the Lord, who is worthy to be praised: so shall I be saved from mine enemies. The sorrows of death compassed me, and the floods of ungodly men made me afraid. The sorrows of hell compassed me about: the snares of death prevented me. In my distress I called upon the Lord, and cried unto my God: he heard my voice out of his temple, and my cry came before him, even into his ears." - Psalm 18:2-6

If you want to understand dad, you need to understand how he was made. Then pray for him. Help him by allowing him to lead. Even when he is broken, he is still a man and needs to lead. God's shoulders are big enough for dad to lean on. He is the heavenly Father for us all. The absolute perfect **go-to** Mr. Fix-it Guy!

CHAPTER 10

UNDERSTANDING A GRIEVING MOTHER

The train has just derailed and lives are blasted all over the place. Mangled steal, burning debris, body parts scattered everywhere with no help in sight. Your entire family was riding this train and the crash location is in the middle of no-where. Desolation. Screaming. Hot Fire. Smoke. You begin to hear the screams and cries of the victims of this crash. Everyone you can see is injured. A crash sight like you've never seen before!

Mom has somehow managed to pry away the jagged debris stuck in her broken body after the crash. She's injured somewhere or everywhere but she doesn't take consideration of her current state as she has already begun the search for her family. She's calling out each of their names one by one. No one answers. She makes her way through the crash sight listening for the sound of familiar cries. She can't see anything except the burning fires. It's pitch black outside.

It will take her quite awhile to locate and visualize every member of her family and their injuries. She recognizes the severity of the crash and sees that everyones injuries are enormous! Mother is going to attempt to pick up every broken piece, repair them and put the train back on the track but **most of all** she will help to mend **each** and **every** wound of her bleeding family.

This is mother's nature, tending to the needs of her family. She will promptly begin her care of everyone without seeking attention for herself. She is the healer and comforter of the family. That's who she is. It is her God-given qualities. She was born with it.

Mom will only focus on the needs of her family. No one will get in her way and if they should try, she will promptly remove them in whatever capacity necessary. There are grave injuries and she will see to it that everyone gets what they need. She's more focused now than ever before to get the help her family needs. Through her clouded and broken state, she will perform each duty like a faithful soldier who has been injured in battle. **She must see everyone of her family out of this wreckage and helped before she will rest.**

Rescue crews will arrive at the scene. They will arrive in the form of EMT's, police officers, fire-fighters, doctors, nurses, specialist, therapist, pastors, family and friends. They arrive to perform their tasks and perform they will. Still, no one will get in mother's way. She's not leaving her family's side. She will refuse attention to her own injuries for now. She's already made a temporary splint for her leg and bandaged the open wounds with what she could find. She has a task, as well, and she **must** perform it! By the grace of God, she will see them all through!

Mother will gain appreciation for so many. Never before has she needed the help of this crew. On the other hand, she will learn to set some strong boundaries. She's about to find out who is for them and who is against them. She's going to learn about all of those "angels in disguise" and discover the truth about the "wolves in sheep's clothing." What a journey to take at such a vulnerable time, but it's the vulnerability that exposes the great lessons she will learn about the people who play an active role in their lives.

As mother makes her way to each and every family member, she becomes challenged beyond her limits in mind, body and spirit. Her spiritual well-being or lack thereof will reflect in her actions/responses. Her actions will reflect her state of mind. Let me explain.

If mother is placing her faith in God, her spiritual resource lacks nothing. God will give her all the strength she needs to have peace of mind. That peace of mind is responsive with righteous actions. But if mother is placing confidence in herself, a medical staff member or anyone else, she will come up empty-handed. Humans are subject to imperfection and placing confidence of any kind into another human-being will result in failure. This failure during such a crash of life will bring results that are unstable and are subject to change like the wind. Mind failure = Spiritual failure = Body Failure.

If mother's resource is anything or anyone other than God Himself, she is going to crumble under pressure. Have you ever placed a teapot on the stove and waited for its signal of whistling when it's ready? Mother is under a significant amount of pressure and the "whistling" will not be pleasant if she has placed confidence in failing resources.

As I attended the funeral viewing service of my dear mother in January of 2007, I was placed under severe anguish. The grieving itself was enough pressure, but the thought of standing near her dead body for eight hours was causing me to become very anxious. While attending prior funerals, I avoided the

116

bodies of the deceased. This time, I couldn't really avoid it and I was very concerned of what she may look like.

My heart was pounding and I was feeling sick at my stomach as we pulled into the funeral home parking lot that day. Quietly, I asked God for strength. I opened my little, pale-blue Bible in hopes to get some Scripture to help me, quickly! To my surprise, I didn't have to read and read to find what I was looking for that day; immediately a few words of a verse at the top, right-hand side of the page stood out. The words were, "Thy Faith Hath Made Thee Whole."

I could have leaped out of my skin with excitement and joy at that very moment! God spoke directly to my heart with those few Words. He was saying to me, "Heather, you already have everything you need to endure this time. You have Me and thy faith (in Me) hath made thee whole!" Goosebumps and tear-filled eyes even now just in recalling this as I write. And ten years later, here I am. I endured that day with the promises God had given me. Little did I know how many more dark days I would live beyond it including the death of my child.

Placing confidence in others words or deeds will always lack somewhere, eventually. A doctor's words or actions will lack because he/she can only go by medical experience, knowledge or resources, all of which have a **limited** supply. A pastor can bring peace and comfort through promises of Scripture, but pastors have a life outside of ours. They can't walk next to us twenty-four hours a day and seven days a week for the rest of our lives. A pastor's calming words are also limited with time. A friend, neighbor, co-worker or family member can be there for us in great ways but are also limited with the demand of their own lives. They aren't super-human and must also live a life beyond our situation. Prescription medications, alcohol or other mind-altering drugs are also limited; there is a limited supply or a limited amount of what can be accessed or taken.

No matter whom or what we may turn to, there is going to be limits outside of God. God is the only resource that is available all of the time and without fail. The stipulation is the application. God must be activated in our lives through faith. It is our responsibility to apply the promises of Scripture into our lives through our faith in God, but, praise God, that faith has an endless supply! Amen!

Understanding mother during this time of darkened nakedness is quite simple; her heart is ripped out of her chest and lying helplessly on the ground for all to see it. She's broken —— torn ——- anguished. And yet she will perform in her motherly way the best she can, tending to every one of her brood. Daily she will attempt to keep it all together and if she has placed her confidence on the Rock of Ages, she will come out of this a better woman, but not without the fight of her life!

The chorus refuses to flee my thoughts, so I will share it with you in writing. *"Rock of Ages, cleft for me, let me hide myself in thee; let the water and the blood, from thy wounded side which flowed, be of sin the double cure; save from wrath and make me pure."* If you know this chorus, I encourage you now to take a moment to sing it. If you don't know it, look it up online and listen to someone sing it. Praising brings healing. If you know Jesus and He is your Savior, then you have gotten a healing of your soul in overcoming death. Praise will bring healing to your life as you live it. When you are ready for healing on this side of Heaven, you will find yourself singing praises to an Almighty God as you weather the storm from Hell. Burdens are lifted at Calvary, Jesus is very near (another wonderful hymn)!

Mom? Dad? Whomever is reading this chapter/book, I applaud you for taking the time to do so. Are you trying to understand her? Mother, are you trying to understand yourself? Pray. Pray for him. Pray for each other. Hold on. Each day beyond grief is new and challenging but it is another day lived beyond it. You won't have to live this day over again.

Help each other. Love each other. Try to understand each other. Remember the faithful saying, "Hurt people, Hurt people."

119

People who are hurting, tend to hurt others in their hurt. We say and do hurtful things in anger; it's what we as humans do. It is common human nature, but in the end love remains faithful. If you will love each other through this —— that love will bloom into something more beautiful than you could imagine! **When love is tested, it is strengthened.** Strengthening is growing. Growing is glowing and glowing love is quite beautiful! Love, that glows in the world for all to see! You can't miss it! It's quite bright! And when you seem to think your love is running dry or dim just remember the Source of which it came! For God so loved the world! Cling to the Rock of Ages and your love will never run dry. The Source of this love has an endless supply! "For God so loved the world, that He gave His only begotten Son, that whosoever believeth in Him should not perish, but have everlasting life." - John 3:16 Oh, the many wonderful and beautiful promises of His love!

Folks reading this chapter on understand her, please make note: the greater the love, the deeper the loss. Mothers are given a quality of tender loving care like no other being on the planet. I guess, then, it is God that gives us that bond that we possess of a mother and her child. When mothers are living what they were created by God to do they are lovingly and tenderly caring for their young. I like to think of true mothers as nurturing treasures. There is nothing they won't sacrifice to help their families, so when the *train* derailed and lives were shattered and displaced it was mother making her way through the rubble in search of her family. Finding each one and tending to them one by one, ignoring her own state of brokenness. **And if her love was great, her losses were greater. If you understand this, you will understand her.** I've heard it said, "It takes a strong woman to be a mother, but it takes a stronger one to be a grieving mother."

CHAPTER 11

THE GRIEVING CHILD

Children grieve the loss of a sibling. How deep their grief will be depends on how full the love is in each home. In our home is great love and when our daughter died, my children experienced great loss and deep grief.

Our oldest child, Maelea (May-Lee), was nearly fifteen when her sister, Grace, died. Her grieving has been probably the most subdued. She's a quiet griever who has dealt well in her grieving, but she would tell you that our prompting to talk about Grace's death has helped her enormously through this process. She's the least likely to bring it up but has always been able to express her grief well in words and tears. She is the big sister. She has displayed great love to each of her siblings throughout her years, so her loss was quite significant. Her leadership in our home is highly recognizable and it's impact has been seen in pleasant ways through each of her siblings and their battle with grief. Because her influence is so well received amongst her younger siblings, her handle on grief has reflected well on our other children.

Our second child, Heidi, turned thirteen less than two weeks before Grace died. Her most difficult birthday, yet, was lived that year. Heidi's love for others, slightly exceeds each of her siblings. Therefore, her grief, I believe, was felt the greatest of all our children. She was the most likely to come to us for comfort. Her tears have been many and her understanding of God's plan has likely been the least recognized. I believe Heidi still searches more than each of the other children for the reason, *why* this happened. Why did Grace, die? Why was she born that way? I believe Heidi may often still ask God, "Why?"

Our third child, Taylor, turned eleven the same month Grace died. She also would attribute her most difficult birthday to have been lived through that time. Taylor is our most compassionate child. She is the one who experiences pain while watching others face it. She aches when she sees those that she loves, ache. Her grief reached beyond her own; she grieves for all of us while she is grieving the loss of Grace, herself. She is also our most quiet child, but has been quick to grieve when prompted. Because grief exceeded beyond herself and she's our quiet child, Taylor did much grieving, alone.

Our fourth child, Joshua, turned nine years old just before we delivered our twins. I feel that I'm still (three years later) working to help him grieve; to get to the place where we are in our grieving. We talk and he grieves, but I believe he is still trying to place this grief in perspective; what it actually meant to him. He was old enough to understand but too young to grasp its depth.

Joshua is one of the kindest and gentlest boys I've ever known. He is our sweetheart with great love and compassion towards others. His grieving has been very real but difficult to pinpoint. He was at such an *in-between* age that he can't seem to understand fully how deep the grief has been for him so the early, initial process of grief is requiring more time. I think because of his age and gender, it may take several more years to reach the place in grief that I am comfortable. As his mother, it is something that I actively attend to.

Our fifth child, Karen, was three when Grace died. She was too young to really understand it. Though she participated in the funeral services and was present at the hospital the day Grace died, I think it was all a (sort-of) make-believe world for her. In some ways it didn't seem real to her —— then. I attribute this to her age. I don't believe her little mind was capable at that time to really understand, much less, to grieve.

As the years have now passed, Karen has begun to grieve more apparently. She is often caught singing the song "Amazing Grace," while playing, alone. Recently, while sitting with our family in the living room, Karen broke down in tears and passionately stated, "I always knew she was there because I felt she has always been with me; even after she died." To hear her at age seven describe it with such expressive passion and pain —— not a dry eye could be found in the room. Her grief was delayed, but it came.

Our sixth child, our son, Gauge, is Grace's twin brother. At the time of completion of this book, he is nearly four years old. Gauge has Down Syndrome (DS/Trisomy 21). He also suffered a severe stoke, as an infant, during open-heart surgery. Currently he is experiencing more seizures. His seizures were, initially, prompted by the brain injury from the stroke; a blood clot went to his brain during the heart surgery. Gauge, because of his multiple health challenges, is also terminally ill. His form of epilepsy is expected to progress, but no one (but God) knows when that will be.

His comprehension of life and death is different than ours, but not less. Allow me to elaborate. Gauge may have significant breeches in his comprehension but he is (by no means) less of a life. He is (by far) the most loved person in our home, quite simply, because he is so very easy to love! Love, is life! Life, is only really lived by having love! Gauge defines love through his life so very, very fully! He did not experience the grief in the loss of Grace, but I believe he did experience the loss when he was separated from Grace.

My children have been grieving since Grace died. As parents, we are responsible for our children's care. That care includes their mental well-being which includes grief and how they are dealing with it. That grief, sometimes includes the grieving of a sibling, a child; a brother or a sister. This is a significant loss for children.

As their mother, I am aware that I notice things that their father wouldn't; he has also acknowledged this. Many times my husband has stated how thankful he is that I notice things with our children, including their state in grief. Mom's, I think eighty-five percent of the help needed for grieving children, falls in your lap. Dad's just aren't made to pick up on things like we do. Women are gifted with an amazing intuition. That intuition puts a greater responsibility on mom at times like these. Love will activate this intuition. But along with that intuition comes a soft voice with a soft touch. Comfort.

So, the question of the hour: "What do you do to help a child grieve?"

WHAT DO YOU DO?

1.) LISTEN

The Bible tells us, "…for out of the abundance of the heart the mouth speaketh." -Matthew 12:34b. This verse tells us how to recognize the condition of one's heart, by listening to what they say. Words are a reflection of a heart's condition. If you want to know how your child is dealing with grief, simply listen to what they say. Mom's and dad's can do this, but as a mother we are gifted beyond that. Let me explain.

A week or so ago, my husband and I were sitting together in our living room talking when one of our children walked in and sat down. Within about fifteen seconds, I asked that child, "What's wrong?" She turned to me and laughed and said, "You always know, don't you." My husband looked at me with some disbelief and said, "She didn't even say anything." I replied, "She doesn't have to. I know my children." Perfect example of a woman's intuition.

When a mother carries that little person inside of her own body for those nine or so months, delivers to nurture and tend to them in every way (diaper changing, breast-feeding, nose-wiping, boo-boo nursing, tear catching, head-kissing, feet cleaning, potty teaching, clothes dressing, appointment reaching, food fixing, merry-maid working, medicine distributing, lullaby singing, heart meshing, hair brushing, food testing, alarm setting, schedule keeping, homework teaching, ball-practice coaching, music lesson landing so you can rest ——- to do it all again) she tends to get to know her child quite well. Better than others. So, it's not out of the ordinary for a mother to first notice a change in her child's demeanor or behavior. Mom's and dad's need to work together to help a grieving child, but it's likely mom who's going to pick up on grief's unspoken silence. However, so much of a child's condition in their grieving can be discovered by listening to what they do say. That should be done by both mom and dad.

As a parent or counsellor works to help a grieving child, their goal should be the same, to get the help that child needs. Bring the help to them. Meet them where they are; wherever that may be. This will require sacrifice. Some children will need more help than others and the others may need more help at a later time of life.

Mom's and dad's, be willing to overlook your own grief in order to help your child. It's easy to wallow in self-pity. It is easy to know how badly you are hurting, but it takes a selfless parent to notice the grief of their child. Just as you are grieving, your child is also. They may not speak specifically about it or boldly *act out* on it, but they **are** grieving as well. All children experience the loss of their deceased sibling, and no matter the age will grieve that loss for the rest of their lives.

Grieving ends the day we are no longer separated from the deceased. That will be when, I hope, we all join them in heaven. My hope is that you, too, will be there with them one day. (Read the chapter "Let the Healing Begin" to learn how you can go to Heaven.)

Each of your children will grieve differently. I got the approval from my children to share what little I did personally about them in this book. Because they each grieve the loss of their sister and we (my husband and I) love them so very much, we constantly evaluate where they are in their process. I know, we've missed noticing things. We don't evaluate everyday, but we have always paid close attention to changes in their behaviors on purpose and have always listened when they needed to talk.

Get your child to talk about how they feel. If this is a foreign concept to your child, you will have a more challenging time getting them to talk. My family has been sharing our feelings openly for years. Any member of the family can vent feelings through words one-on-one or in a family setting. For those who are trying to help a grieving child, listen with your heart, eyes and ears; on purpose. If you do, their pain will not go unnoticed and the help will come by those they love. Listen. You aren't the only one who is grieving this deep loss.

2.) COUNSEL

The very, first place a child needs to be taken to is the Word of God. The Word of God tells us "Where no counsel is, the people fall: but in the multitude of counsellors there is safety." -Proverbs 11:14. God tells us in His Word that a multitude of council is best. Much counsel is needed for the safety of our children in their grief. Notice also what happens **where there is no counsel,** *"the people fall."* If you want your children to have success in the overall process of grief, they need counsel; much counsel. **(THE WORD OF GOD BEING THEIR PRIMARY COUNCIL.)** The council may come from having many counsellors (many people) or much council, meaning they are receiving a lot of counseling but not necessarily from many counsellors (persons).

Each of these counsellors need to be on the same page. What you *don't* want to have is one counsellor telling your child about what the Bible says, such as, Heaven with it's mansions and streets of gold, while another counsellor says, "Well, Heaven is an imaginary place. We will all go to a place of peace and rest but some people have a different way of believing where or what that actually is." NONSENSE. Keep their counsel on the same page! Grieving is difficult enough. Don't tell them about God and Heaven and then allow someone to discount the truth! Don't tell them about Heaven and forget to teach them about the God of Heaven and how they can get there themselves. <u>God forbid their council ever conflicts the Word of God.</u>

In my opinion, their counsel doesn't have to be a licensed counsellor, it can be a list of parents, pastors, grandparents, Sunday School teachers, friends, family members and may include licensed professionals. It is highly recommended that you get someone included in this "multitude of safety" who deals with this frequently or as their profession such as a bereavement counsellor or pastor. I understand that up until the last century, there were no licensed counsellors yet many people received the help they needed through *unlicensed* counsel; a multitude of safety! However, it is best to include someone who does deal in regular grief counseling.

3.) DIRECTION

Though you may listen to them and also get the multitude of counsel they need, it is the direction that you point them that matters the most. "But my God shall supply all your need according to his riches in glory by Christ Jesus." - Philippians 4:19 Dear folks, if you and your children are rich in Christ, your every need will be supplied, including the need in the void grief brings. The absence of that individual brings about the grief that we feel. According to the Eternal Living Word of our Almighty and Gracious God, every need will be fulfilled through Christ Jesus. **Going to Christ doesn't remove the void, but it fills the void.**

Dear mom and dad, quite simply, if a parent struggles greatly in their grieving, so will those that live with them; their children. If you aren't getting the help you need, neither will they. No matter how large your need is, Christ's supply is greater! It is as if you, in grieving, are able to tap into a Fountain of Healing with endless supply. Do you and your children need help in this loss? Make Jesus your Fountain and never thirst again. *He is* all the help you and your grieving child will ever need, the Go-To Source on which we can TRULY lean on!

*LISTEN

*COUNSEL

*DIRECTION

CHAPTER 12

LET THE HEALING BEGIN

I recently attended the funeral of a four-year old little girl named, Maddie. After the funeral service was over I made my way over to her mother. As I stood in line behind other folks who sympathized for this family, I tried to think of something to say. I couldn't think of anything that seemed right for that time. Every statement or thought that came to mind seemed so *generic*. It wasn't enough. What could I really say?

I wanted to say something to help, but I felt that I couldn't do that at this time. As I approached my friend (the little girl's mother) I looked her in the eyes and quickly hugged her. It was a strong and somewhat lengthy hug. As I started to let go, I pulled back, grabbed her hands and looked her in the eyes. With tears full, I knew at that moment she saw my shared grief. We looked at the pain present through each other's eyes just for a moment as the tears flowed. I knew she could see that I understood the level of grief she was feeling that day. I could relate to her pain. I believe in a strange way (though I said nothing to her) I brought comfort to her through my presence. She knew the woman she looked eye-to-eye with had also lived a day like she was now living.

I wanted to say or do something that could take this pain away from her; any portion of it! However, I knew I couldn't do that. I was nearly three years removed from that very day I had lived through myself. I knew the grief of my friend had reached a depth that I understood, and, therefore, nothing I could say was going to remove what she was experiencing in this awful time of her life.

I wanted to sit her down and go over all the things I had experienced and what I had learned from it. I wanted to just *zoom* her through that season so she could be on the other side of it. I wanted that season to be i*n the past* for her; to be over! However, I knew that her daughter was sent to their lives for many reasons. God had different plans for Maddie and those she would influence with her life.

Though some of the reasons (I'm sure) were similar, they wouldn't be exact. God presents great detail through each life. All of these details are far beyond my understanding and too great in number to count! Secretly and privately there was a "classroom" of life that reached beyond my friend, Melissa, and her family. Little Maddie's life-purpose reached beyond her parents and siblings. Her beauty and detail exceeds any human description! What every life has to offer, goes beyond what any of our minds could ever grasp!

My friend, Melissa, and her family were given a very special gift of life. That gift was taken from this earth and has left a hole in their hearts! So, how does healing begin? How does one live without someone who brought such beautiful detail and joy to our lives? It begins by the recognition of God in each life.

God has a purpose for each life from the moment we enter this world, He has a plan for us. A plan we can not see. If we don't first recognize the Creator of the Universe, His Son, Jesus Christ and His Majesty of being the God of All, we will not begin to heal. We will continue to remain broken in a state of grief that leaves us feeling as though that child/person will remain absent forever.

God has a design set in motion. A design set for each of us to reach our life's purpose and fulfill our potential. God knew that in Maddie's life, only four years would be needed for her to fulfill its purpose. He knew only two months would be needed for our daughter, Grace, to reach her full purpose.

137

This life is temporary for all of us. In God's grand design in creating mankind there was no death. But, mankind was given a free-will and sin entered this world thousands of years ago. Because of sin, there is now death. Because of Christ there is no need to have an eternal separation from God through that death. Jesus makes it possible for each of us to gain a home in Heaven with our Heavenly Father, someday.

The moment Maddie took her last breath and her body experienced that physical death, she immediately became present with the Lord. Maddie had never denied God. She had never knowingly sinned against Him, therefore repentance wasn't necessary for Maddie. Because she did not knowingly sin, she herself never created a distance between her and God. Maddie, was born His child, remained His child and went to Heaven to continue living as His child. She never was away or astray from God. She never knew what it was like to not be a child of the KING! (I hope you found an AMEN in your heart somewhere while reading that!)

At birth we are all born God's children. The day we knowingly sin against God is the day we put an eternal separation between He and us. That eternal separation is then set in motion. It (Hell) then becomes our destination at the end of this life. But, if we repent, we change our destination. One day we will either be with God in Heaven or eternally separated from Him in Hell ——— Heaven or Hell ——— each of us ——— one day. (So, how is this supposed to bring healing to you? Keep reading.)

Hell is an eternal separation from God. It is where people exist eternally without God. In Matthew 22:13b the pain of Hell is expressed with these words, "…there shall be weeping and gnashing of teeth." Hell is an eternal lake of fire, that **is real death.** Experiencing a physical death here on earth is one thing, but to be eternally separated from all that is good, (God) is a place called Hell, where Scripture tells us is a "second-death." Revelation 21:8 "But the fearful, and unbelieving, and the abominable, and murderers, and whoremongers, and sorcerers, and idolaters, and all liars, shall have their part in the lake which burneth with fire and brimstone: which is the second death."

Currently, even the unbelievers are experiencing God's goodness here on earth because they have not yet experienced the second death. While they live, they still have opportunity to change their fate. While alive we are all blessed because God created the universe and it is His air we breathe. It is His beauty we see in the lives of others and His wonderfully, DETAILED, designed-with-perfection creation! Joy is experienced here. Love is experienced here. Life is lived and shared here! In Hell there is no love because there is no God. There are no mountain streams, no ocean waves crashing on the sand and no laughter. No hugging or kissing in Hell —— no joy of any kind in any form ———- no, not in Hell —— zero joy there —— only pain and REAL DEATH!

Hell is pain. **It is a final death.** It is a literal lake of fire. No changes can be made once you reach it. There are no passports, no tickets out of Hell. It is **a** FINAL destination in the eternal lake of fire where you never die. You forever burn —— ——conscious and aware —— very much alive ——forever!!! We can't even comprehend what forever actually means. The best description I can think of in our finite minds is that it simply never ends. That is a very long time to be in a place of pain, having no love, no beautiful scenery, no God and no joy. NO PEACE, forever!

Here on earth, God is present everywhere even the deepest jungle. In Hell, He is NO-WHERE to be found! That is a final death. What the Bible calls a second death. It is the one that takes place after the physical death. It is only experienced by those who deny the **One, True and Living God.** This second death is an eternal (too late to change your mind) separation from God! Revelation 2:11 "He that hath an ear, let him hear what the Spirit saith unto the churches; He that overcometh shall not be hurt of the second death." Let's find out exactly what that "overcometh" means. (Continue on reader, you're just getting to the real "Place" of healing.)

In our healing, we must recognize God and His eternal plan. Once that recognition is presented to us and we accept it, we can pick up our *Ticket* to Heaven, **Jesus Christ.** If we have Him, we now have everything needed to escape that second death. Recognize God the Father, His Son and His Spirit. They are all working together AS ONE in the healing of your mind, body and soul.

In order to recognize God and His plan, we need to understand a few things about death here on earth. Remember in previous chapters of the book we discussed how death was never God's intention? He did NOT create mankind to die. It was the sin of mankind (each of us) that changed His plan and brought death. Romans 5:12 "Wherefore, as by one man sin entered into the world, and death by sin; and so death passed upon all men, for that all have sinned." So when sin entered into this world, death also entered. Remember the story from Scripture about the specific day that sin entered? (Adam and Eve's sin in the Garden of Eden.) God had told them that they could eat of every tree except the fruit of the one tree and Satan came as the form of a serpent, tempted Eve to disobey God by the eating of that one fruit and she ate it. She fell from grace. Sinned. She and Adam both, and they knew immediately. (We all know when we've done something wrong.) SATAN WAS PRESENT IN THE WORLD, even back then.

Where did Satan come from? Did God create him, too? (God did create all things.) The answer is, yes, God did create Satan. However, when God created Satan, He created Him as a beautiful and powerful angel in Heaven. Satan **was** an angel of Heaven and was also given leadership there over the choir. He was Heaven's choir director at one time, but when he became envious of God and wanted to have God's power ——- he was kicked out. When Satan was kicked out, he left with power and his talents in music. He maintains those capabilities today in this world. He's quite good at music. He's actually quite good at everything he does because he has been at his hellish, wicked schemes for a few thousand years now. Many refer to him as the death angel.

Ephesians 6:12 says, "For we wrestle not against flesh and blood, but against principalities, against powers, against the rulers of the darkness of this world, against spiritual wickedness in high places." Every single one of life's battles are because of Satan's presence in this world. **One day, God will bring it all to an end.** The plan is laid out in Scripture and Satan knows, very well, what God's plan is. He knows that his time is limited here on earth. He knows that he is truly hell-bound with no possible way to turn his *rig* around. (Not the case for you, reader.)

Satan is working to take as many souls as he can with him to his final destination, that eternal lake of fire, HELL. He has become very good at his tactics (remember, he has been doing them for a few thousand years.) Strange, Isn't It? How Satan gets so many people to blame God for death? Maybe that is why Satan (the devil) is often referred to as the master deceiver. *"Be sober, be vigilant; because your adversary the devil, as a roaring lion, walketh about, **seeking whom he may devour:"** I Peter 5:8* However, the Bible tells us in First-John 4:4b "... greater is He that is in you, than He that is in the world." We know Satan is "he that is in the world." The part of that verse "He that is in you" is Jesus Christ. This passage was written to believers. Believers have Jesus Christ; they have accepted Him and He is their Savior and Jesus is the answer to overcoming Satan and his tactics of trying to get us to join him in Hell! (Have you ever noticed what you get when you remover the letter "d" from devil?) Each and every hardship, death included, Jesus is the answer to the healing! The Overcomer! Yes, Jesus is still the answer!

Jesus is the One Who can and will heal our broken hearts! Jesus has given us the capability through faith to endure hardships! John 4:15 says "Whosoever shall confess that Jesus is the Son of God, God dwelleth in him, and he in God." We need God *in* us to overcome Satan. We receive that dwelling of God inside of us when we confess who we are and who Jesus Christ is! Jesus is the mediator between God and man, the middle-man, so to speak. Without Him, we would have no avenue to get to God.

Cleansing is needed to come before the throne of God the Father, so God the Son (Jesus Christ) made a way to receive that cleansing. This cleansing of our soul is done by simply asking Him (Jesus) for the cleansing. Romans 10:9 "That if thou shalt confess with thy mouth the Lord Jesus, and shalt believe in thine heart that God hath raised him from the dead, thou shalt be saved." <u>Salvation is a redemption received by us through Christ.</u> We are redeemed (saved) from sin and Hell. We can only be saved from Hell through the cleansing given to us by Jesus Christ. We are not only delivered from that lake of fire, we are also given a home in Heaven!

When we accept Jesus as our personal Lord and Savior, we are then cleansed of all unrighteousness. It is a complete washing, and God (in the form of HIS SPIRIT) enters our life. He dwells inside of us! It is then that the "greater is He that is in you" part of that verse can be lived out to overcome Satan "he that is in the world."

When the day came that we chose to sin against God, we became hell-bound and a Spiritual battle began over not just our life here on earth but also a battle of our soul's eternal destination. If we go through life without Christ, it is as if we are on the battle front without any armor. No armor = No help! However, receiving Christ into our lives gives us every piece of the armor needed to confront Satan here on earth, but best of all the deliverance from *HELL*.

Satan was present in the Garden of Eden that day tempting Eve. Satan had power and he had knowledge. He used those clever powers to tempt Eve (and Adam), therefore sin and death entered this world. Satan is the reason we are tempted to sin and he is the reason we experience death. He is the reason there is a literal Hell which is the second death we will suffer **IF** we do not have Jesus Christ as our *ticket* to Heaven. Christ is our escape from Hell and our Entrance to Heaven.

Satan will do his best to even prevent you from reading this book. Why? Because of the truths proclaimed with Biblical confidence. The Words of God Almighty, HIMSELF through the Scripture shared in this book! Those truths shed light on a dark path. Those truths solidify who Satan is, what he aims to do and why he wants you to believe his lies. He simply doesn't want you to know the truth about Christ. He wants you to end up in the eternal lake of fire *with him*.

Instead, you've made it this far in reading this chapter about healing. If you accept Jesus Christ as your Lord and Savior, you can begin living by the faith God has given through His Son, **overcome** Satan and his lies against God receiving the peace which passes all understanding! Eternal Peace. Heaven-bound!

For my friends, Mike and Melissa, the healing of the loss of their daughter began with God the Son, Jesus Christ. It is in Him that they found peace in God the Father and His plan for each of their lives including, Maddie's. It is then that death becomes not the end but rather the beginning. The beginning of a new life of permanent joy and peace, never experiencing death again! It is **in Christ** that they also have wisdom in this battle of their lives and have become over-comers. As for their daughter, Maddie, she never had a losing battle against Satan! She beat him every time!

I don't know where you (reader) are, but if you now realize the significant battle you are in and you don't have the Armor of God, I strongly encourage you to accept Jesus Christ into your life, today! He is where the Healing begins. You can pray something to Him like this, "Dear Jesus, I know Who You are. I know You are the Savior of the world. I believe through You I can overcome death by having eternal life with You in heaven. I know I have sinned against You, many times. I confess to You, today, that I am a sinner. I ask that You would forgive me of each and every sin! Jesus, forgive me of all my unrighteousness! I ask You, now, to enter into my life as my Good Shepherd to Comfort and Guide me each step of the way, through every battle I will face! I thank You for your love and forgiveness. And, Lord, I thank You for my home in Heaven, someday. Help me on my journey until then. I need You, Jesus. Amen." **Let the Healing Begin.**

CHAPTER 13

FINDING GRACE IN LIFE AND DEATH

I waitressed at a local truck stop when I was in high school. (I know! I still can't believe my parents allowed me to do that.) I was taking a smoke break while at work one day, (I don't have that harmful habit anymore) and while sitting in the break room a co-worker came in to also take a break. Somehow, God came up in our conversation. He didn't believe in God but he knew that I did.

He went on to talk about how God wasn't real because He allows too many bad things to happen. In the same conversation he spoke about ouija (wee-jee) boards and his style of music, heavy metal. His dress style was very dark as well, but I always spoke to and treated him the same as I did everyone else. I think he respected that.

During our conversation that day I said something like this, "Chris, the opposite of daylight is darkness. The opposite of black is white. The opposite of up is down. The opposite of good is evil and the opposite of God is Satan. That being said, I believe you have experienced enough in life to know that evil and darkness definitely do exist and therefor the opposite is true! You just spoke about your experiences with the ouija board ——— which is darkness. Since you are aware of the darkness, undoubtably, you know there is LIGHT, and *there indeed is a God up in Heaven right now!*"

He looked as though he had seen a ghost. It was the first time in my life that I had ever said anything that changed the countenance on someone's face so dramatically. Weather or not he ever allowed it to sink in, I do not know, but I do know that what I said changed something inside of him. The truth never returns void, my friends. His expression said it all.

I share this story to prompt each of you to the knowledge that we all do indeed have that tug in our hearts of Who God is! The more we begin to "see," by faith, Who God is, the more evident Satan will become. But you don't have to take my word for it. Right now, in your heart, I know you can feel it. It's a working beyond this world. It is a Spiritual work.

It is the work of opposites in the Spiritual world. The *work* that says, "I'm not reading anymore of this non-sense. This girl is clearly off her rocker! She's a nobody and some stupid person gave this book to me anyway. I was just bored or desperate, that's why I'm reading it. There is no way God is real, I agree with that co-worker she had. If God was real, then why do so many bad things happen?" The opposite *work* that also says, "Man, I really feel this strange pull. It's like there's someone else here in the room with me, now. I've been searching for these specific answers and reading this has given me some clarity I really needed. It's helped me. Surely, with the fact that I have been given this book, God is real! He has used these words to speak to me, today, specifically. He knows how much I really needed this. He knows what my questions were before I got this book and He knows the path that I was taking. He's trying to save me!"

Spiritual Work. It's currently active in your life right now. You are reading a book that has taken me over three years to write. It is my very first book. One that I had no desire to ever live or to write about. Finding Grace ——— in life and death. You are alive and currently reading this book because your child died or is dying. Found any Grace, yet? I pray you can now see the real struggle in life and death. If you can, you will find the grace that I once found when I was lost and you, too, can say, "Amazing Grace, how sweet the sound that saved a wretch like me. I once was lost, but now I'm found; twas blind but now I see!"

The day before our daughter died, a team of her doctors set up a conference for all of us to meet in discussion over our plans for her future. (She had been living all of her days here on life support.) During that meeting we learned that even if she gained the weight to receive her heart surgery, the surgery couldn't be performed. Her heart defects where so significant that it wasn't medically possible to repair her heart ——- ever. In fact, on a scale of 1-10, her heart defect was rated a 10 (being the worst) by every cardiologist we spoke to.

I'm not sure why it took sixty days to get this type of clarity, but I do trust God with it. I can say, with confidence, that the loss is greater because I knew her and spent time with her. She was no more or less my daughter without that time but a greater bond and connection was formed by living some life with her. Therefore, I can certainly say, this book wouldn't exist without those sixty-one days. Maybe that is the reason! So, then, (dear reader) do you understand that my suffering was greater because of her sixty-one days but those days were needed to bring this book to you? **There is a bigger plan than what we can see.**

After the conference meeting with Grace's team of doctors, my husband and I drove home and spoke together openly about our thoughts. We both agreed that keeping her alive was now for us and not for her. "Why should she fight to live for one more day?" we thought. So, we made a decision to take her off of life support. We didn't want her to die in the hospital without us being there. It was also vitally important to us that we were present with her when she died. Knowing that she lived daily facing death and was suffering, we decided to *let her go.*

With bold confidence through my faith in God, I walked into the room of the hospital the next day knowing that if God wanted Grace to live, she would be healed. In all reality, we weren't making that decision of life or death for her, God was. As her loving parents, painfully, we walked her to the gates of Heaven and let her go.

It was a peaceful home going. A room of friends, loved ones, some medical staff, her dad and I gathered to send her HOME. Her nurse, Kasey, handed her to me, wrapped in a heart- themed pink afghan. Kasey was giving Grace breath's through a ventilator bag. Grace had been given some medication to keep her calm and pain-free in case she should struggle in her breathing. I held her close to me, facing her dad. The vent bag was removed. No more breaths were given to her.

I kissed her, watched her face and sang a couple songs, including, "Amazing Grace." Some family and friends joined-in as I sang it. Her nurse came over to check for a heartbeat; she still had one. The room was silent. Her dad and I just stared, shed tears and waited for God to take her home.

I began to sing "our song." If you've read this book, you would know that Grace and I had a song of praise to God. It was titled, "How Can I Keep from Singing" by Jamie Leigh. (You can google to find it.) I sang her our song, and sometime during the course of doing that, Grace went to Heaven. Her nurse came over shortly after and confirmed that she had no heartbeat. She was gone.

My greatest fear in life was lived that day. Ironically, I was praising God in song when Grace went to Heaven and not just any song, our song. She went from hearing her mother sing to hearing the angels of Heaven singing as they welcomed her, HOME!

My child had died. I cried all day that next day, the eeriest cry that I have ever heard to this day. Grief is hard. The grief for a child is especially hard. I always knew that if I had to face it, that it would be the worst thing I could ever experience on this earth. The literal lake of fire, Hell, would be the only thing that I believe could be worse although, this grief is a Hell on earth blasted from the spine of Satan himself.

I am writing this book because there are others who have faced this hurt, just like me. As fulfilling as it has been to write this book, I have had to relive all of those deep wounds again and again, knowing much of what you (reader) have felt. But God appointed me to do this, of that, I am confident.

Today, I wrap it all up with this chapter to finish the book; Finding Grace in Life and Death. I found it. Grace. It was God's Amazing Grace. It was He that lead us to name our daughter, Amazing Grace Browning. It was He that loved us through every part of our journey in grief and it was He that understood each pain. It was God that loved us through it all and He that put a song of praise in my heart to share with my daughter during her short time here with me. No One else in the whole, wide world knows how deeply hurt we are to have let her go, No One but God. He knows —— every ——- single ——- heart ——- ache!!!!

It was also God that lead me to write this book. Every detail. His Amazing Grace is enough. "And He said unto me, My Grace is sufficient for thee: for My strength is *made perfect* in weakness. Most gladly therefore will I rather glory in my infirmities, that the power of Christ may rest upon me."

-II Corinthians 12:9

I hope each of you have found more of His Grace, in life and in death; God's Amazing Grace!

"AMAZING GRACE"

Amazing Grace, how sweet the sound,
That saved a wretch like me.
I once was lost but now I'm found,
Was blind, but now I see.

'Twas grace that taught, my heart to fear.
And grace, my fears relieved.
How precious did that grace appear,
the hour I first believed.

Through many dangers, toils and snares,
I have already come.
'Tis grace that brought me safe thus far,
and grace will lead me HOME.

When we've been there ten thousand years,
bright shining as the sun.
We've no less days <u>to sing God's praise</u>,
than when we first begun.

THOSE THAT I WOULD LIKE TO THANK:

I would like to thank my husband, Josh, for his inspiration and encouragement given to me to write this book. "Thanks for always standing by me and believing in me! I don't think you could ever know just how much I've needed you through all of the stormy seasons life has brought us. You are my only. I love you, oh, so much!"

I would also like to thank my grandparents, Brad and Alice, for their model of love passed down through my mother, Karen, and now to me. "I'm forever grateful for your continued love and support. My words could never come close to the thanks my heart feels! I love you both! You are the most amazing couple I've ever known!"

The Walker Family: "I don't know what we would have done these last few years without you all! Your love and support through the *thickest* of times has meant more than you will ever know! How could I ever thank you for being there? I love you all, whole bunches! Thank you."

My children: "Your love in return of mine is a precious and priceless gift! I will never take it for granted! You are my favorites!"

My pastor, Michael, and my dad, Harry, for their emphasis on The Word of God and Its influence in my life. "Thank you both for your faithfulness of instilling The Word of God in me. Truth permeates my mind because of each of you. I love you both."

Jack and Sandy, "Your countless visits to fill in for me at the hospital, the rides given to my children to and from the hospital and your faithful prayers lifted us beyond measure through our darkest season of life. Thank you both! We love your family!"

Mike and Melissa, "Thank you for your blessing in allowing me to share some of your story and for being a friend to me and my family. We love you all, and we are blessed to have known sweet, Maddie."

Angie Sampson, "Your editing skills are amazing! I'm so thankful I had someone so close to me who understands my thinking to review the work God placed in me. Thank you for your friendship to my mother and my family! Love you!"

Sylvia, at Johnson Printing, Eliot Maine: "Thank you for all the much needed help on the cover of the book and for your prayers! God bless you! We were blessed to know your son, Jack. Love to you all."

To my sister, Mendy, "Your daily visits to see my babies will forever mean so much! Thank you. I have always loved you!"

New Hope Baptist Church Members: "Thank you for tending to my family through it <u>ALL</u>! Your love and prayers exceed! May God richly bless each of you! I love you all!"

Last, and, certainly not least, my life coach, Kim. "God placed you perfectly in our lives at just the right time! Your Godly counsel gave us what we needed to continue being who we were before all of the madness and to see the great potential that God has for us! Thank you. I love you."

www.ingramcontent.com/pod-product-compliance
Lightning Source LLC
Chambersburg PA
CBHW032111040426
42337CB00040B/177